Ready-to-Use

VIOLENCE PREVENTION SKILLS
LESSONS & ACTIVITIES

for Secondary Students

 RUTH WELTMANN BEGUN
and
FRANK J. HUML, Editors

THE SOCIETY FOR PREVENTION OF VIOLENCE

 JOSSEY-BASS
A Wiley Imprint
www.josseybass.com

Published by Jossey-Bass
A Wiley Imprint
989 Market Street, San Francisco, CA 94103-1741   www.josseybass.com

Library of Congress Cataloging-in-Publication Data

Ready-to-use violence prevention skills lessons & activities for
    secondary students / Ruth Weltmann Begun and Frank J. Huml, editors
    ; The Society for Prevention of Violence with The Center for Applied
    Research in Education.
        p.   cm.
    Includes bibliographical references (p.   ).
    ISBN 0-87628-917-0
    ISBN 0-7879-6691-6 (layflat)
    1. School violence—United States—Prevention—Handbooks, manuals,
    etc.   2. Conflict management—United States—Handbooks, manuals,
    etc.   3. High school students—United States—Handbooks, manuals,
    etc.   I. Begun, Ruth Weltmann.   II. Huml, Frank J.   III. Society
    for Prevention of Violence (Ohio)   IV. Center for Applied Research
    in Education.
    LB3013.3.R43   1998
    371.7'8—dc21   97-47478

FIRST EDITION
HB Printing 10 9 8 7 6 5 4 3 2

ABOUT THIS VIOLENCE PREVENTION SKILLS TEACHING RESOURCE

Today's educators carry added responsibilities because significant social changes have had an impact on human relations. Family ties have been loosened. The number of single-parent families has grown. Stresses in many families are often high. Thus, young people are frequently exposed to influences that tend to make them aggressive and possibly violent. Moreover, television, now in almost every home in the United States, frequently shows events not suitable for guiding our young. Juveniles who cannot read and write watch violent scenes and might draw wrong conclusions. Children are very adept with computers and thus are able to surf the Internet for programs not suitable for their age. Unless schools, other social agencies, and parents counteract the media and other asocial influences as preventive means, verbal and physical interpersonal abuse and violence will be an increasing problem.

This volume is designed to serve as a companion to the four-volume series entitled "Ready-to-Use Social Skills Lessons & Activities" developed by The Society for Prevention of Violence. It contains fifty (50) lessons and associated activities focusing on topics such as stimulant use, family relationships, dealing with anger, and gang-related activities. These contemporary topics are well suited to today's classroom.

The lessons are presented in a uniform format and follow a Structured Learning approach to teach the skills. They focus on real situations in children's own lives, such as dealing with feelings, self-esteem, peer pressure and respect for others, and are readily adapted for use in any classroom, school or home setting.

The ideas, stories and scenarios for most of the lessons and activities were developed by experts in the following fields: domestic violence, drug abuse, alcohol abuse, juvenile crime, gang activity, psychology, social skills, and conflict resolution. Part of the project was funded by the Aetna Foundation. Most of the funding came from The Society for Prevention of Violence, a non-profit organization founded by the late Semi J. Begun, Ph.D., and his wife, Ruth Weltmann Begun, M.S., and sponsored by them and various contributing corporations and foundations, including the Semi J. and Ruth W. Begun Foundation. Specific credits are given on the Acknowledgment page.

Major objectives of teaching these lessons are to build students' character and help them develop the understanding and skills necessary to deal with difficult and violence-threatening situations in ways that lead to settlement of conflicts and grievances through communication without recourse to violence. I believe that such training can be effective and successful by preventing the use of violence. Thus, students will benefit from the practice of violence prevention skills throughout their lives.

Ruth Weltmann Begun, M.S.
The Society for Prevention of Violence

ACKNOWLEDGMENTS

This curriculum, serving as a companion to the four-volume "Ready-to-Use Social Skills Lessons & Activities" series, was developed under the direction of Ruth Weltmann Begun, president, and Frank J. Huml, executive director, of The Society for Prevention of Violence. The following persons served as advisors and consultants to the project:

Nancy Corvo, consultant

Donna Gilcher, teacher, Berea Children's Home, Cleveland, Ohio

Janet Macklin-John, consultant

William Stencil, psychologist, Cleveland Public Schools, Ohio

Kenneth Trump, president, National School Safety & Security Services,
   Cleveland, Ohio

Byron Wasko, assistant principal, East Cleveland City School District, Ohio

Their expertise provided contributions to the content of the lessons. The editors are sincerely appreciative of their willingness to serve and contribute to the development of this companion teaching resource.

The Society is also appreciative of the continued cooperation of Mr. Winfield Huppuch, vice president of Prentice Hall Direct, a division of Simon & Schuster.

The Society for Prevention of Violence also gratefully acknowledges the financial support of The Aetna Foundation for the development of the material within this curriculum. This development was made possible through the direct efforts of Mr. Douglas Ganim, regional manager of the Cleveland office, who initiated a FOCUS Grant by The Aetna Foundation. The provision of this grant demonstrates Aetna's continuing commitment to the well-being of our society.

ABOUT THE SOCIETY FOR PREVENTION OF VIOLENCE (SPV)

The Society for Prevention of Violence (SPV) is dedicated to reducing the prevalence of violent acts and asocial behaviors in children and adults through education. It accomplishes this mission by teaching children and adults the use of the skills necessary to build their character, helping them acquire a strong values system, motivating them to develop their communication skills and to realize growth in interpersonal relationships. The mission includes integration of social and academic skills to encourage those who use them to reach their full potential and contribute to our nation's society by being able to make decisions and solve problems through effective and appropriate means.

As a non-profit organization, the Society had its origin in 1972 as The Begun Institute for The Study of Violence and Aggression at John Carroll University (Cleveland, Ohio). A multitude of information was gathered, studied, and analyzed during the ensuing ten-year period. Symposia were held which involved numerous well-known presenters and participants from various career fields. Early on, the founders of the Institute, S. J. and Ruth Begun, foresaw the trend of increasing violence in our families, communities, and across the nation, and chose to take a leadership role in pioneering an educational approach to help alleviate aggressive and antisocial behavior. The educational approach was and continues to be the sole *PROACTIVE* means to change behaviors. Current conditions reflect our society's reliance on reactive means of dealing with this problem. During the next ten-year period, through the determination and hard work of Ruth Weltmann Begun as executive director, the workshops, parent training sessions, collaborative projects, and a comprehensive (preschool through grade 12) Social Skills Training Curriculum were developed.

Today, classroom teachers in numerous school districts across the country are utilizing this internationally recognized curriculum. The Society continually seeks support through individual donors, grants, direct paid services, and material/consultant service sales. It also has expanded its involvement in the educational process by:

- publishing a semiannual newsletter, a resource catalog, and other pertinent material;

- providing in-service training for professional staffs of schools, parents and others;

- providing assistance in resource identification, proposal writing/project design and evaluation;

- tailoring instructional (academic and other) delivery designs to specific school/organization needs;

- implementing pilot demonstration projects with foundation support;

- offering graduate level workshops in cooperation with and through John Carroll, Kent State, and Ashland Universities in the area of teacher training (credits earned in these workshops may be applied toward renewal of certificates through the Ohio Department of Education);

- presentation of professional workshops for graduate credit, such as: Teaching Social Skills in the Classroom, Violence Through the Ages, Classroom Management, Gangs, Guns, Drugs and Violence, Domestic Violence, Family Dynamics, etc.;

- offering a graduate level credit "self-study" workshop, *Teaching Social Skills in the Classroom*, in cooperation with Ashland University (OH) to non-Ohio residents nationwide; and

- continued development of new workshops and other related and pertinent projects.

As we move into and through the twenty-first century, we must work diligently and cooperatively to turn challenges into success.

For further information, contact The Society for Prevention of Violence, 3439 West Brainard Road #102, Woodmere, Ohio 44122 (phone 216/591-1876) or 3109 Mayfield Road, Cleveland Heights, Ohio 44118 (phone 216/371-5544/45).

ABOUT THE VIOLENCE PREVENTION SKILLS CURRICULUM

Philosophy

We believe that the learning of certain life skills is the foundation for social and academic adequacy. It assists in the prevention of asocial behavior and leads to successful functioning and survival skills for our citizens. Social behavior and academic behavior are highly correlated. We believe it is more productive to teach youth the proper ways to behave than to admonish them for improper behavior. This requires direct and systematic teaching, taking into consideration social and developmental theory in the affective, cognitive, and psycho-motor domains. Learning should be sequential, linked to community goals, and consistent with behaviors that are relevant to student needs. This violence prevention skills curriculum is based on these beliefs and is closely associated in concept and format with the comprehensive preK-12 Social Skills Lessons and Activities curriculum developed by The Society for Prevention of Violence and published by Prentice Hall.

Curriculum Overview

As young people mature, one way they learn social and peaceful behaviors is by watching and interacting with other people. Some who have failed to learn appropriate behaviors have lacked opportunities to imitate good role models, have received insufficient or inappropriate reinforcement, or have misunderstood adequate social experiences.

The last decade has presented great challenges to young people and classroom teachers alike. The prevalence of weapons, drugs, alcohol, and ever-increasing family disintegration along with the reduced influence of the community-at-large have contributed to increased anti-social behaviors on the part of juveniles.

The Violence Prevention Skills Lessons and Activities curriculum closely resembles the Social Skills Lessons and Activities curriculum developed by The Society in its format, lesson structure, and philosophy. It is intended that this curriculum will be utilized as a complement to the social skills curriculum. The curriculum is designed to provide real-life situations for students to react to by using suggested skill components and by role playing and teacher modeling of the skills. The teacher and the rest of the class then provide positive reinforcement to encourage the continued use of the appropriate skills in situations that will occur in any environment.

Teachers using this curriculum can be flexible. The curriculum is designed to be used in the classroom as lessons taught for about 20-30 minutes, two or three times a week. However, it is not the intent that these be the only times violence prevention skills are taught and learned. Every opportunity should be used to reinforce, model, and coach the youngsters so that they can practice the skills often enough to feel comfortable with them as part of their ways of thinking and behaving. Therefore, the teacher should remind the students of the skills and the need to use them in all appropriate situations once the skills have been demonstrated. The teacher should also plan to model the skills in any and all interactions with the youngsters. The teacher should be *consistent* in not only using the skills when they are taught, but in using them in all interactions with the students. Only this kind of consistent modeling will assure that the youngsters will see the skills used repeatedly and begin to know and feel comfortable with using them. Teachers should also adapt the material to class needs and design and develop strategies, models, and interventions other than those suggested here. Students can even be involved in helping to develop modeling strategies and other techniques.

Structured Learning consists of *four basic components:* modeling, role playing, discussion of performance, and use in real-life situations. For more effective teaching, the lessons include eight steps that follow a directed lesson format (see below):

Behavioral Objective: The expected outcome of learning the social skill that can be evaluated.

Directed Lesson: Each behavior is defined and stated in observable terms; the behavior is demonstrated and practiced; a student's level of performance is evaluated and inappropriate behaviors are corrected. Positive reinforcement is used to encourage continued use of the skill in all areas of the student's environment.

1. **Establish the Need:** The purpose of teaching the lesson is included. What benefits will learning the skill provide? What are the consequences of not learning the behavior?

2. **Introduction:** Stories, poems, puppets, and questions are used to make the social skill more concrete to the children.

3. **Identify the Skill Components:** These skill steps are used to teach the behavior. By following and practicing these steps, the student will be able to demonstrate the behavior when needed.

4. **Model the Skill:** The teacher or socially adept child demonstrates the appropriate behaviors so that the students can imitate them. The skill components are referred to during the modeling.

5. **Behavioral Rehearsal:** The children are given an opportunity to perform the behavior which can be evaluated, corrected, and reinforced.

   A. *Selection*—The teacher selects participants or asks for volunteers. The number of children depends on the time allowed and whatever is appropriate for each lesson.

   B. *Role Play*—The participants are assigned their roles or situations they will role play.

   C. *Completion*—This is a means to determine that the role playing is complete. After each role play, reinforce correct behaviors, identify inappropriate behaviors, and re-enact role play with corrections. If there are no corrections, role play is complete.

   D. *Reinforcers*—Positive reinforcement by the teacher and the class is used for maintenance of the skill. Various methods can be used: verbal encouragement, tangible rewards, special privileges, and keeping a record of social and academic improvement.

   E. *Discussion*—The student's level of performance is evaluated and inappropriate behaviors are corrected. How did the participants feel while performing? What difficulties might be faced in implementing the skill? What observations did the class make?

6. **Practice:** Activities that help the children summarize the skill. The practice can be done by using worksheets, doing art projects, making film strips, writing stories, keeping diaries and charts, and so on.

7. **Independent Use:** Activities that help facilitate the use of these behaviors outside the school environment. Family and friends take an active role in reinforcing the importance of using these alternative behaviors in a conflict situation.

8. ***Continuation:*** At the end of each lesson, the teacher reminds the class that applying these skills can benefit them in academic and social relationships. Stress that although there are difficulties in applying the skills (such as in regard to negative peer pressure), the benefits outweigh the problems. One such benefit is more self-confidence in decision-making. Maintaining social behavior is an ongoing process. It requires teachers to show appropriate behaviors and reinforce them when they are demonstrated.

STRUCTURED LEARNING

FOUR BASIC COMPONENTS

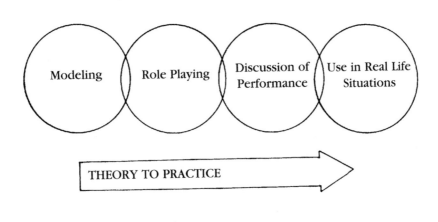

We believe that such training can be effective and successful by increasing understanding and the development of appropriate thought processes and skills to avoid conflict which might result in violence in the students' lives.

BIBLIOGRAPHY

Apter, Stephen J. & Goldstein, Arnold P. (1986). *Youth Violence: Program and Prospects*. Needham Heights, MA: Allyn & Bacon.

Barnett, O. W. & LaViolette, A. D. (1993). *It Could Happen to Anyone, Why Battered Women Stay*. Thousand Oaks, CA: Sage Publications.

Bart, P. B. & Moran, E. G. (eds.) (1993). *Violence Against Women*. Thousand Oaks, CA: Sage Publications.

Begun, Ruth Weltmann (1995). *Ready-to-Use Social Skills Lessons and Activities*, grades pre-K. West Nyack, NY: Center for Applied Research in Education.

Begun, Ruth Weltmann (1995). *Ready-to-Use Social Skills Lessons and Activities*, grades 1–3. West Nyack, NY: Center for Applied Research in Education.

Begun, Ruth Weltmann (1995). *Ready-to-Use Social Skills Lessons and Activities*, grades 4–6. West Nyack, NY: Center for Applied Research in Education.

Begun, Ruth Weltmann (1995). *Ready-to-Use Social Skills Lessons and Activities*, grades 7–12. West Nyack, NY: Center for Applied Research in Education.

Buzawa, E. & Buzawa, C. G. (1996). *Domestic Violence*. Thousand Oaks, CA: Sage Publications.

Byers, G. H. (1994). *Collaborative Discipline for At-Risk Students*. West Nyack, NY: The Center for Applied Research in Education.

Cartledge, Gwendolyn & Milburn, Joanne F. (1986). *Teaching Social Skills to Children*, 2nd ed. Needham Hts., MA: Allyn & Bacon.

DeJong, W. (1994). *Preventing Interpersonal Violence Among Youth, An Introduction to School, Community, and Mass Media Strategies*. Washington DC: U. S. Department of Justice.

Edel, W. (1995). *Gun Control*. Westport, CT: Praeger Publishers.

Elias, M. J. & Tobias, S. E. (1996). *Social Problem Solving*. New York, NY: Guilford Press.

Fox, R. E. (1996). *Harvesting Minds*. Westport, CT: Praeger Publishers.

Frances, R. J. & Miller, S. I. (eds.) (1991). *Clinical Book of Addictive Disorders*. New York, NY: Guilford Press.

Frank, I. C. (1996). *Building Self-Esteem in At-Risk Youth*. Westport, CT: Praeger Publishers.

Furlong, M. J. & Smith, D. C. (1994). *Anger, Hostility and Aggression*. Brandon, VT: Clinical Psychology Publishing Co., Inc.

Gelles, R. J. & Cornell, C. P. (1990). *Intimate Violence in Families*. Thousand Oaks, CA: Sage Publications.

Goldstein, Arnold P. (1991). *Delinquent Gangs*. Champaign, IL: Research Press.

Goldstein, Arnold P., Apter, Stephen J. & Harootunian, Berj (1984). *School Violence*. Englewood Cliffs, NJ: Prentice Hall.

Goldstein, Arnold P. et al. (1980). *Skillstreaming the Adolescent: A Structured Learning Approach to Teaching Prosocial Skills*. Champaign, IL: Research Press.

Goldstein, Arnold P. & Conoley, J. C. (1997). *School Violence Prevention*. New York, NY: Guilford Press.

Goldstein, Arnold P., Harootunian, B. & Conoley, J. C. (1995). *Student Aggression, Prevention, Management and Replacement Training*. New York, NY: Guilford Publications.

Goldstein, Arnold P., Reagles, K. W. & Amann, L. L. (1990). *Refusal Skills*. Champaign, IL: Research Press.

Hampton, R. L., Jenkins, P. & Gullotta, T. P. (eds.) (1995). *Preventing Violence in America*. Thousand Oaks, CA: Sage Publications.

Hanson, D. J. (1996). *Alcohol Education*. Westport, CT: Praeger Publishers.

Hoffman, Allen M. (ed.) (1996). *Schools, Violence and Society*. Westport, CT: Praeger Publishers.

Holinger, P. C., Offer, D., Barter, J. T. & Bell, C. C. (1994). *Suicide and Homicide Among Adolescents*. New York, NY: Guilford Press.

Holmes, G. R. (1995). *Helping Teenagers into Adulthood*. Westport, CT: Praeger Publishers.

Huff, C. R. (ed.) (1996). *Gangs in America*. Thousand Oaks, CA: Sage Publications.

Kirk, W. G. (1993). *Adolescent Suicide*. Champaign, IL: Research Press.

Lal, S. R., Lal, D. & Achilles, C. M. (1993). *Handbooks on Gangs in Schools*. Thousand Oaks, CA: Corwin Press.

Mannix, D. (1989). *Be a Better Student: Lessons and Worksheets for Teaching Behavior Management in Grades 4-9*. West Nyack, NY: The Center for Applied Research in Education.

Mannix, D. (1991). *Life Skills Activities for Special Children*. West Nyack, NY: Center for Applied Research in Education.

Mannix, D. (1993). *Social Skills Activities for Special Children*. West Nyack, NY: Center for Applied Research in Education.

McGinnis, E. & Goldstein, A. P. (1984). *Skillstreaming the Elementary School Child: A Guide for Teaching Prosocial Skills*. Champaign, IL: Research Press.

Morley, E. & Rossman, S. B. (eds.) (1996, August). *Education and Urban Society*. Thousand Oaks, CA: Corwin Press.

Nastasi, B. K & DeZolt, D. M. (1994). *Schools Interventions for Children of Alcoholics*. New York, NY: Guilford Press.

Pagliaro, A. M. & Pagliaro, L. A. (1996). *Substance Use Among Children and Adolescents*. New York, NY: Wiley.

Patterson, G. R. (1975). *Families*. Champaign, IL: Research Press.

Peled, E., Jaffe, P. G. & Edleson, J. L. (eds.) (1995). *Ending the Cycle of Violence—Community Responses to Children of Battered Women*. Thousand Oaks, CA: Sage Publications.

Pernanen, K. (1991). *Alcohol in Human Violence*. New York, NY: Guilford Press.

Bibliography

Petersen, S. & Straub, R. L. (1992). *School Crisis Survival Guide*. West Nyack, NY: The Center for Applied Research in Education.

Pfeffer, C. R. (1986). *The Suicidal Child*. New York, NY: Guilford Press.

Poland, S. (1989). *Suicide Intervention in the Schools*. New York, NY: Guilford Press.

Reiss, D., Richters, J. E., Radke-Yarrow, M. & Scharff, D. (eds.) (1993). *Children and Violence*. New York, NY: Guilford Press.

Silverman, M. M. & Maris, R. W. (1995). *Suicide Prevention*. New York, NY: Guilford Press.

Stephens, R. (1995). *Safe Schools: A Handbook for Violence Prevention*. Bloomington, IN: National Educational Service.

Stephens, R. D., Exec. Director (1990). *Gangs in Schools*. Malibu, CA: National School Safety Center.

Stephens, T. M. (1978). *Social Skills in the Classroom*. Columbus, OH: Cedars Press, Inc.

Walters, C. D. (1994). *Drugs and Crime in Lifestyle Perspective*. Thousand Oaks, CA: Sage Publications.

Ward, C. (1995). *Attitudes Toward Rape*. Thousand Oaks, CA: Sage Publications.

Wheeler, E. D. & Baron, S. A. (1994). *Violence in Our Schools, Hospitals and Public Places*. Ventura, CA: Pathfinder Publishing.

Wieke, V. R. & Richards, A. L. (1995). *Intimate Betrayal*. Thousand Oaks, CA: Sage Publications.

CONTENTS

VIOLENCE PREVENTION SKILLS LESSONS AND ACTIVITIES FOR SECONDARY STUDENTS

| *Lesson* | *Violence Prevention Skill* | *Page* |

Contents

Contents

VIOLENCE PREVENTION SKILLS LESSONS AND ACTIVITIES FOR SECONDARY STUDENTS

TO THE TEACHER

This section presents fifty (50) ready-to-use violence prevention lessons with a variety of related activities and worksheets.

The lessons may be used in any order you desire, though they are sequenced in a broad way, beginning with general strategies for everyday life. Ultimately, of course, you will match the needs and ability levels of your students with the particular lessons and learning objectives. It may be necessary to repeat some of the lessons several times over the course of the school year.

The activity sheets accompanying these lessons may be photocopied as many times as you need them for use with individual students, small groups, or the whole class. You may also devise activity sheets of your own to enrich and reinforce any of the lessons.

Violence in Our Society

Crime and violence have become commonplace in our society. The last decade has seen significant increases in juvenile violence. Such increases can only portend our future as a nation. In spite of our leadership in technological and scientific areas, we have not demonstrated the same understanding and acceptance of responsibility in addressing the needs of our youth.

- 3.6 million persons in our population are addicted to drugs.

- More than one-third of all high school seniors say they engage in heavy drinking.

- The arrest rate for violent juveniles is expected to nearly double from current levels in the years ahead.

- 83% of juvenile detention center inmates reported owning a gun as did 22% of students attending high schools in urban areas.

- Urban schools have chronic gang problems, and suburban areas have emerging gang presence.

- Suicide rates of adolescents are at record levels.

All too often, we have approached problems of violence through legislation rather than education. Tempting as it might be to seek a simple, perhaps even curable biological cause, a large body of evidence points to violence as a learned behavior. From the earliest ages, children learn by observation, practice, and continual reinforcement.

Helping Youth Unlearn Asocial Behaviors

The school's role in combating, and preventing, violence can be a powerful one: helping young people unlearn aggression and asocial behaviors by substituting constrictive learnings about cooperation, caring, understanding, and social skills for solving problems. A former surgeon general stressed that we must take an interdisciplinary approach to reducing violence. Among her prescriptions for violence prevention are incorporating violence prevention into the school curricula through teaching social skills. Resilient youth usually possess the four attributes of social competence, problem solving skills, autonomy, and a sense of purpose and future.

It is important to realize that the teaching of social skills is a primary prevention program which targets entire populations of youth in the development of skills that reduce the probability of the initial onset of problems. Such learnings are of prime importance and longest lived in terms of a continuum of prevention which also includes secondary and tertiary approaches.

Training for Life

The violence prevention skills curriculum in this volume closely parallels in structure, format, and methodology the curriculum in the companion four-volume Social Skills Lessons and Activities series. Primary elements of each lesson include modeling (the skill is presented by an adult role model), role play (behavioral rehearsal or practice for future use of the skill), and performance feedback (praise, approval, and encouragement are given for the appropriate display of the target skill). Topics related to substance abuse (drugs, alcohol), gangs, weapons, psychological problems, and family harmony are presented in ready-to-use lessons which can be supplemented/enhanced in many ways by the creative teacher.

These lessons become universal life skills training. For many schools, the addition of social skills and prevention programming may seem to be another "drain" on the teacher's day. Yet elementary and secondary educators, and key adults in the community (social service agencies, parent groups, outreach groups, and religious groups), are the first line of defense in our nation's attempt to curb violence.

We believe that the use of this material can be effective and successful in improving discipline, reducing the dropout rate, and teaching youth to cope with adverse feelings in a peaceful manner. Thus, students will benefit from violence prevention skills as well as from related training such as teaching of social and other life skills throughout their lives.

Making Proper Decisions

Behavioral Objective: The students will learn how to make proper and well-thought-through decisions. This experience and knowledge is most important to succeed in life and to meet its challenges head-on.

Directed Lesson:

1. ***Establish the Need:*** The importance of youth learning to make decisions in order to face life's challenges in a rational and methodical manner cannot be overlooked. Frequently, decisions are made on impulse or without forethought as to the consequence(s). Such decisions often lead to grief, frustration, and failure. It is important that youth, at the earliest age, develop those thinking skills required to make proper decisions in meeting the challenges of maturing and succeeding in life.

2. ***Introduction:*** The teacher reads the following scenario to the class:

   Judy is a teenager of fifteen who is well liked by many of her classmates. She is talented and a good student. Her parents (Tom and Anne Smith) are supportive of her and encourage her in the pursuit of academic scholarship and extracurricular activities. As an attractive teen, she is admired by a number of the boys— one of whom is Matt, a potential dropout. Matt has been known by persons in his neighborhood to have broken into at least three neighbors' homes or cars to steal in order to support a "habit." The neighbors, while discussing the events openly, have not filed charges because of Matt's mother's prolonged illness and his father's stature in the community (minister). Judy's mother has often expressed her desire directly to Judy that she not associate with him.

   One afternoon, near the end of the school day, Matt meets Judy at her locker during the change of classes and asks her to join the group of boys (including himself) for an "after school party" at his home. Being cautious, she asks if his parents are aware of the party; he indicates that his parents are in Florida for a brief vacation, but that they are aware of it.

   Remembering her mother's concern, she calls home and tells her mother that the cheerleading team, of which she is a member, has been called to an "emergency" meeting after school. Her mother understands and instructs her to come home as soon after the meeting as possible. Judy agrees. She then meets Matt at his locker at the end of the school day and attends a party.

   Coincidentally, the cheerleading advisor phones Judy's home to inform her mother that there will be a meeting following the close of school the next day. Judy's mother asks if this is a meeting in addition to today's and is told that there was no meeting *today* . . . .

3

3. *Identify the Skill Components:* List the following skill components on the board.

1. Identify the problem.
2. Define your goal.
3. Think of as many solutions to the problem as you can.
4. For each potential solution, consider all consequences.
5. Choose your best solution.
6. Rethink the solution a few more times.
7. Make a decision.
8. Act upon your decision.

4. *Model the Skill:* The teacher will ask one student to role play Judy and the teacher will role play Judy's mother. After confronting Judy for having given a fake excuse, the teacher portraying Judy's mother will use the skill components to show Judy how they could have helped her make a better and more proper decision.

5. *Behavioral Rehearsal:*

A. *Selection:* Select three pairs of students for three role plays.

B. *Role Play:* Have one pair of students role play Judy and Judy's mother from the introductory story and another pair of students role play a conversation between Judy and Matt, in which Judy makes a different decision in her reaction to Matt's invitation. Have the third pair of students enact the following role play. (All students should keep in mind the skill components.)

> **Your best friend has decided that he or she wants to spend more time with a group of people at school who are known to use alcohol and other contraband stimulants. This friend asks you to join them at the park after school to use contraband stimulants. Using the decision-making skills, decide what you will tell your friend about meeting him/her after school and about this group of friends and their use of contraband.**

C. *Completion:* As each role play is finished, students led by the teacher will determine if appropriate behaviors were used. If not, the role play should be reenacted with corrections; if yes, the role play is complete.

D. *Reinforcers:* Acknowledge your appreciation for the efforts and cooperation of the role players and invite applause by the class.

E. *Discussion:* Start a discussion by asking the following questions: What is the difference between an impulsive decision and a decision made through careful thought? Can you share with us a story when you made an impulsive decision and tell us what resulted? How could a thought-out decision have helped?

6. *Practice:* Divide the class into three groups, A, B and C, then distribute the following worksheet, "Decisions," and assign one of the three problems for decision-making to each group. Assign problem A to Group A, and so on. After the three groups have completed this exercise, have the class discuss their decisions and the thinking process that was required to come to a unanimous decision in each group.

7. **Independent Use:** Distribute copies of the worksheet entitled "Making an Important Decision" for the students to do at home and return in one week for discussion in class. Recommend their use of the skill components in this essay assignment.

8. **Continuation:** Throughout the year, the teacher will reinforce the skill by pointing out that the decision-making process must be continually practiced and refined since it is frequently necessary in adult life to make a well-thought-through decision immediately.

Name _____ Date _____

DECISIONS

Directions: Each group is to respond in writing, giving their solution to the problem and explaining how they applied the skill components to arrive at their solution.

SCENARIO A

You share a locker with a very popular student at school. Before school one morning, you open the locker and discover a small plastic bag with something in it that you think looks like marijuana. You must decide how to speak to your locker partner about your discovery. You did not want to jump to conclusions about the contents of the bag and why the bag is in your locker, but this locker also belongs to you and you share responsibility for its contents.

SCENARIO B

Using alcohol or other drugs is forbidden on your school sports team, and you agree with this policy. Two of your team's best players begin bragging to you and other teammates about their use of drugs before games, claiming that their athletic performance is enhanced by the drugs. You and other nonusers on the team must decide how to approach this problem; the health of your friends as well as the success of your team is at stake.

SCENARIO C

A parent for whom you are babysitting comes home drunk and wants to drive you home.

Name _____ Date _____

MAKING AN IMPORTANT DECISION

Directions: Write an essay about an event in your life in which an important decision had to be made. Describe the decision that was made, explain the thinking process that helped you to arrive at the decision, and tell why this was the best decision.

When you have finished the essay, discuss it with your parents or another adult and write down with whom you discussed the essay and his/her reaction.

Learning to Be Tolerant

Behavioral Objective: Students will learn to be tolerant of others who have physical and/or mental disabilities or are obviously very different.

Directed Lesson:

1. **Establish the Need:** Unless specifically taught to show kindness and respect to persons who are different from them or disadvantaged due to physical and/or mental disabilities, young people sometimes ridicule, show cruelness, and even do physical harm to such persons since they do not understand their needs. Some youths do not want to associate with disabilities in any way. Students need to realize that persons with disabilities of all ages require companionship, the opportunity to communicate and participate in a variety of activities, and are eager to give and receive friendship. A tolerant, supportive, or participatory relationship with such a person will prove beneficial to both parties since it will increase self-esteem and confidence and promote the sharing of knowledge and talents.

2. **Introduction:** The teacher will use the following story to introduce the skill:

   Tom was short and extremely overweight. He wasn't built for exercises and for games which required agility and speed. However, he refused to be left out of any gym class activities. His attempts to do even simple exercises often caused the rest of the seventh grade boys to shake with laughter; he was the subject of many jokes. Though Tom was usually unsuccessful in his attempts at physical activities, he never quit.

   Tom was pleasant to his classmates and was willing to help them with academic problems whenever they asked for his assistance.

   Today, in gym class, one of the activities was to jump over a "horse." When it came to Tom's turn, he prepared to give it a try. His classmates were teasing him as usual, saying "Tom's too fat to jump over the horse," and "Look out horse, here comes fat Tom."

   Tom got the best running start he could. Just as he jumped, one of his classmates, Ed, moved the "horse." Tom crashed to the floor with a sickening thud. As he lay on the floor, the hurt and furious anger he felt was evident on his face. The gym class was silent. . . .

   After a pause, the teacher will elicit answers from the students to the following questions/statements:

   ▶ **Why was the class silent?**

Handwritten annotations at top of page:

is there such a thing as an "innocent bystander" in these situations? No Passive Supporter.

by not speaking up, we are saying it's ok —

Is it hard to stand up to a group? or a pop. person? yes!

But There is strength in numbers.

> ▶ **Describe how Tom is feeling.**
> ▶ **How do you think Ed is feeling?**
> ▶ **Is there anything that anyone could have done to change the situation which led to this?**
> ▶ **What is a disability? Was Tom disabled? (A student might be asked to find a definition of disability in the dictionary, or the teacher can present a definition.)**
> ▶ **What can be done to show tolerance toward persons with disabilities?**
> ▶ **Are disabilities always permanent?**

3. ***Identify the Skill Components:*** List the following skill components on the board:

1. Realize the many forms of disability.
2. Know what tolerance means.
3. Understand that people do not ask to be disabled.
4. Treat persons with disabilities as equals.
5. Realize everyone's need to be accepted by others.
6. Show tolerance through the choice of words and actions.
7. Encourage others to be tolerant.

4. ***Model the Skill:*** The teacher can develop his/her own modeling example or use the following one: Mr. Smith has just completed the seating assignment, in ink, for a new class. A new student is brought to the room by the office assistant with a message from the principal that the new student needs special placement in the class due to poor eyesight.

The teacher will role play Mr. Smith and use the skill components to show how they can help to develop tolerance towards a person with a disability.

5. ***Behavioral Rehearsal:***

A. *Selection:* Select four groups of 4–5 students.

B. *Role Play:* As time permits, give each group an index card on which one of the following situations requiring tolerance has been written. The students within each group are to pick one of their members to portray the person with a disability while the others act as the classmates. Each group will develop the verbal and physical interactions needed to make the story complete.

– A group of students is waiting on a corner to cross a busy intersection. A blind person with a cane approaches. There is a barrier on the sidewalk around a hole. Try as he/she might, the blind person can't seem to find his/her way around the barrier.

– A new student has entered the class. She is from India, does not speak English very well, is dressed in her native attire, and eats a lunch that looks and smells very different from what the other students are accustomed to.

– Billy is the class "nerd." He tells everyone how things should be done, gets all A's, dresses like a businessman every day, and brags about all the places he has been. Billy is an only child. His parents are very busy with their own careers and have never spent a lot of "quality" time with Billy doing "family things." Billy gains their attention and approval because of his intelligent mind. Despite his outward appearance and different behavior, Billy does have a great sense of humor.

– Use the story about Tom from the Introduction, leaving out the last two paragraphs.

C. *Completion:* The teacher and students will decide whether the role play was correct and whether the skill components were properly applied. If there is need for correction, re-enact the role play. If there are no corrections, the role play is complete.

D. *Reinforcers:* Each group should receive praise from the teacher and peers for their participation in the role plays.

E. *Discussion:* After each role play, use the following questions to encourage discussion about the skill:

▶ **Is it easier to be tolerant of someone who is paralyzed or someone who is overweight? Why?**

▶ **Are there different degrees of tolerance? Explain.**

▶ **Is being "different" (in manner of dress, speech, physical looks, etc.) a disability?**

▶ **How can the skill of being tolerant be applied to persons who are not disabled but "different"?**

6. Practice: Distribute copies of the worksheet entitled "Name the Disability" for students to complete and share in class.

7. Independent Use: Hand out copies of the log sheet "Disabilities and Differences" which students will use to record observations of persons with disabilities. Students can make their observations around the school, at home, in their neighborhood or any other public place. After about two weeks, a fully completed log sheet should be returned to class and shared. (Students may require more than one log sheet form.)

8. Continuation: The teacher should alert students to situations which may require tolerance and review and use the skills with the students, as needed.

Name _____ Date _____

NAME THE DISABILITY

Directions: Name three different disabilities that afflict people. Explain how each disability might cause them to be excluded from certain activities, friendships and other life experiences, and how this could affect their self-esteem and confidence. Then explain how you could show tolerance for a person with the disability.

Disability #1 _____

   1. How would this disability cause a person to be excluded from activities, friendships, and other desirable life experiences?

   2. How would this disability affect their self-esteem/confidence?

   3. How will I show tolerance for a person with this disability?

Disability #2 _____

   1. How would this disability cause a person to be excluded from activities, friendships, and other desirable life experiences?

   2. How would this disability affect their self-esteem/confidence?

   3. How will I show tolerance for a person with this disability?

Disability #3 _____

   1. How would this disability cause a person to be excluded from activities, friendships, and other desirable life experiences?

   2. How would this disability affect their self-esteem/confidence?

   3. How will I show tolerance for a person with this disability?

Name _____   Date _____

DISABILITIES AND DIFFERENCES

LOG SHEET

Disability or Difference	Where Observed	People's reaction to this disability or difference. Was tolerance shown?	What do you think about the way people reacted?

Responding to Failure

Behavioral Objective: Students will learn how to respond to failure when faced with difficult tasks. They will learn to understand that it is most important to accept failure without acting out in an unruly manner and that unruly behavior is no remedy for failure.

Directed Lesson:

1. **Establish the Need:** Young people often respond to failure when faced with difficult tasks by giving up after the first try or by using the failure as an excuse for unruly behavior. Students need to learn to identify what caused the failure and what they can do to reduce failures. This will help them rationalize that failure is no excuse for unruly behavior and that unruly behavior will not solve any difficulties. Instead they will learn to realize that unruly behavior will lead to more failures and problems.

2. **Introduction:** The teacher will read the following story to the class:

   Brian had difficulty understanding his English class assignments. When the teacher called on him to read in class or answer questions, he would become frustrated and angry. If the teacher forced the matter, he would disrupt the class by acting out in one form or another. After a few days, Brian "cut" English class and started "hanging out" with other cutters, roaming the school halls and hiding out in different places in the school. While hiding out, Brian and the others would smoke, steal food from the cafeteria, and sometimes run around in the neighborhood near the school.

   After reading the story, the teacher will ask the class:

   ▶ **How did Brian respond to his difficulties?**

   ▶ **What consequences might he face for his choice of handling the matter, that is, cut classes?**

3. **Identify the Skill Components:** List the following skill components on the board:

   1. Identify your difficulties.

   2. Accept failure.

   3. Realize that unruly behavior is no remedy for failure.

   4. Determine the cause(s) for failure.

   5. Learn from failure.

   6. Identify resources for help.

   7. Ask for help.

    8. Think positively.

    9. Be persistent in your efforts.

    10. Overcome the difficulty.

4. ***Model the Skill:*** The teacher will relate an experience in which he/she failed and found it was easier to give improper responses than to deal with the difficulty. The teacher, using the skill components, will illustrate how he/she addressed the problem and avoided the consequences by not participating in inappropriate and unruly behavior.

5. ***Behavioral Rehearsal:***

    A. *Selection:* The teacher will ask one student at a time to role play Brian from the story in the introduction, by showing how to react more properly to the failure.

    B. *Role Play:* The students will role play the story in the introduction, using the skill components to address the failure.

    C. *Completion:* After the role play, the teacher will identify any problems and correct the role play, if necessary, and critique how the students used the skill components. If no correction is required, the role play is complete.

    D. *Reinforcers:* The teacher and peers will thank the role players and highlight their use of the skill components by giving verbal and nonverbal praise.

    E. *Discussion:* The teacher will ask the class the following questions:

    ▶ **What consequences could have been avoided by Brian if he had followed the skill components?**

    ▶ **Is it better to be persistent and ask for help in solving problems?**

    ▶ **What are the consequences for unruly behavior?**

    ▶ **Is failure an excuse for unruly behavior?**

6. ***Practice:*** Distribute the worksheet "Pros and Cons" to be completed as a classroom assignment and discussed in class.

7. ***Independent Use:*** Hand out the worksheet "The Wrong Week" for students to complete as homework assignments and ask them to return it in one week to be discussed in class.

8. ***Continuation:*** The teacher will analyze unruly or contrary behaviors by students and identify possible failures that may have been used to rationalize, justify, or exacerbate such behaviors. The teacher will point out that unruly behavior is never to be excused and that failures should be considered opportunities to learn from them to do better the next time. The teacher will emphasize that a positive approach to failure will help to avoid future failures.

Name _____ Date _____

PROS AND CONS

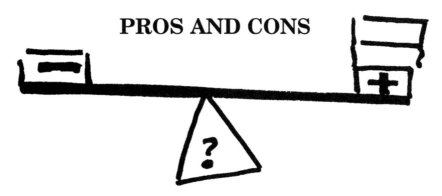

Directions: Answer each of the following questions. Follow the skill components to answer questions 3 and 4.

1. What are your three greatest strengths ("pros")?

2. What are three of your greatest weaknesses ("cons")?

3. How could you improve your weaknesses? Who or what could help?

4. If you get help and you still have a problem, what should you do?

Name _____ Date _____

THE WRONG WEEK

Directions: Think of a week when it seemed that everything went wrong for you. In the space below, explain what happened to you, how you handled the failures, who or what helped you handle them, and what you did to prevent these failures from happening again. (Follow the skill components.)

Describe two failures:

How were the two failures handled?

How did you respond to the failures?

Who helped you or what resources did you use?

How did you overcome the failures?

What steps did you take to prevent similar failures from reoccurring?

Learning to Cope with Life's Problems by Using Social Skills

Behavioral Objective: Students frequently are pressured into joining a group or gang of peers which could introduce them to a life of stealing, lying, and even killing. Sometimes, even if they have decided to do so, it is not easy for a young person to leave such a group and to change his/her life to a more peaceful and productive existence. Students have to learn that the use of social and other life skills can help them remake their lives, and to leave the group.

Directed Lesson:

1. **Establish the Need:** Young people are often tempted and pressured to join a group of peers which is engaged in illegal activities, such as stealing, indulging in stimulants, and even killing for fun and gain of clothes and money. When they become aware of the adverse activities that such a group pursues, they often want to leave the group. However, leaving the group can be difficult for two reasons. One reason is that the group usually applies pressure on the person who wants to leave to convince him/her to remain part of it. The second reason is that the lifestyle of the group provides a sense of "belonging," and it is not easy to find other satisfying activities that give them the same sense of being accepted and part of a group.

   Students will learn that social and other life skills can provide them with the strength to leave such a group and find new satisfactory pursuits in their recreational activities.

2. **Introduction:** The teacher will read this story to the class.

   In English class, the teacher was having the students give oral presentations. The students had been asked to speak about something that had greatly influenced them to stay out of trouble. After a few students had given their presentations, Marcus Banks was asked to give his.

   Marcus began by telling about the difficult times in his life. He told of his one-time exposure to gang life, and even admitted that this had led to his smoking marijuana and other drug usage. He told of how he got the money to buy drugs by stealing from his family and friends. He even threatened to beat up other students if they didn't hand over some money. One day, Marcus was with another gang member. He watched as the gang member stole another person's coat and new athletic shoes and then, for no apparent reason, shot him. Marcus said that as he watched and saw the kid lying in a pool of blood, he knew that if he didn't change his life, he would end up the same way.

Marcus wanted to change his life, but he did not know how to get out of the gang until he, with the help of the teacher or counselor, found out that social and other skills would help him to cope with his situation and build a more promising life.

3. ***Identify the Skill Components:*** Write the following skill components on the board, on a transparency to be used with an overhead projector, or on sentence strips.

    1. Analyze your situation.
    2. Define who you like to be.
    3. Reject negative peer pressure.
    4. Be responsible for your actions.
    5. Be accountable to yourself.
    6. Be honest and straightforward.
    7. Be helpful to others.
    8. Decide if you need help.
    9. Select an adult you can trust.
    10. Join a productive activity of your choice.
    11. Discuss the reasons for leaving with the group.
    12. Prepare for an honest exit.
    13. Change your life.

4. ***Model the Skill:*** The teacher will select one student to role play Marcus, from the story in the introduction, while he/she role plays the teacher and guides Marcus through the thought process of how to accomplish his goal of leaving the gang. To do so, he/she will use the skill components.

5. ***Behavioral Rehearsal:***

    A. *Selection:* The teacher will select four pairs of students.

    B. *Role Play:* All four pairs of students will role play Marcus who wants to leave a group or gang which uses stimulants, steals, etc., and asks the advice of a trusted adult to help him start a new life. The adult will be played by the other student. The scenario of each pair of students should be different, and either the student role playing the youth or the one role playing the adult will use the skill components to find a way out of the student's dilemma.

    C. *Completion:* After each role play, the teacher reinforces correct behaviors, identifies inappropriate behaviors, and asks the students to re-enact the role play with corrections. If there are no corrections, role play is complete.

    D. *Reinforcers:* The teacher will give verbal and non-verbal praise for correct behavior.

    E. *Discussion:* The teacher will start the discussion with the following questions:

      ▶ **Do you all understand the skill components fully?**

      ▶ **How does responsible differ from accountable?**

▶ **Can you think of other skills that could be used, such as, for example, self-esteem, understanding consequences, etc.?**

▶ **What could be the consequences if you stay with such a group as described by Marcus in the story I read to you?**

6. ***Practice:*** Distribute copies of the worksheet entitled "Is This Me?" and have students complete and discuss it in class.

7. ***Independent Use:*** Distribute the worksheet "My Dreams." Ask students to return the completed worksheet in one week and discuss their responses in class.

8. ***Continuation:*** The teacher will emphasize that the use of social and other life skills will empower each of us to cope better with life and be more responsible and satisfied with our lives.

Name _____ Date _____

IS THIS ME?

Directions: Answer the following questions in paragraph form using the given criterions.

Question: Who am I?

Criterion: What values, history, traditions, and cultural precepts do I recognize, respect, and practice?

Question: Am I really who I think I am?

Criterion: To what extent do I have to understand, internalize, employ, and reflect the cultural background of my heritage?

Question: Am I all I ought to be?

Criterion: To what extent do I possess and consciously apply the enduring standards and meanings which measure people in terms of cultural substance and concrete conditions?

Name _____ Date _____

MY DREAMS

Directions: For each topic listed below, describe what you would like to achieve or do in life. Then have one of your parents or your guardian tell you what they hope you will do or achieve and add their answers.

TOPIC	ME	Parent or Guardian
Recreation		
Hobbies		
Profession		
College/ Vocational School		
Sexual Relationships		
Drugs		
Guns		
Family		
Job		

Developing Self-Respect

Behavioral Objective: Students will learn how to develop self-respect and respect for others.

Directed Lesson:

1. **Establish the Need:** Young people need to learn to develop respect for themselves and for others. The lack of self-respect in many youths is evident from their participation in activities such as drug abuse and gang initiations and related asocial behaviors.

   By learning to respect themselves, students will be better prepared to respect others and less likely to join groups who commit illegal acts.

2. **Introduction:** The teacher will lead a discussion using the following questions:
   - **What behaviors would suggest that a young person has little self-respect?**
   - **Why would someone not respect himself/herself?**
   - **Why should you respect yourself?**
   - **Why should you respect others?**
   - **How do you think you can gain self-respect and respect for others?**

3. **Identify the Skill Components:** List the following skill components on the board or on sentence strips:

   1. Identify your physical and personal characteristics.
   2. Identify personal characteristics you would like to improve.
   3. Identify physical characteristics that you dislike but must accept.
   4. Identify "specific" ways you can improve personal characteristics.
   5. Identify how you can "live with" your physical characteristics.
   6. Realize that self-respect requires acceptable behaviors.
   7. Identify behaviors that show self-respect and respect for others.
   8. Exercise such behaviors.

4. **Model the Skill:** The teacher will model the skill by demonstrating how he/she as a professional educator will behave in a manner that shows that he/she has self-respect and respect for others. When reprimanded in front of the class by the principal for not having notified the school that he/she would be late arriving in school that day, he/she will respond in a polite manner fully in control of his/her actions and behavior.

5. *Behavior Rehearsal:*

    A. *Selection:* The teacher will ask three students, and more if time permits, to role play.

    B. *Role Play:* The students will role play themselves articulating their own personal and physical characteristics and showing how they are developing respect for themselves and for others by exhibiting appropriate behaviors. In doing so they will use the skill components.

        If time permits, the teacher will add role plays such as:

        a. A student who stutters will show how to develop self-respect by taking a public speaking course.

        b. A student who is an experienced ice skater, but falls in a public ice show, develops self-respect by returning to ice skating in public.

    C. *Completion:* After each role play, the teacher should reinforce the correct behavior and identify inappropriate behaviors. The students should repeat the role play with corrections. If it was done well and correct, the role play is complete.

    D. *Reinforcers:* The class should applaud all role players. Verbal and nonverbal praise from both the teacher and the class is essential.

    E. *Discussion:* The teacher will solicit and encourage students to discuss questions about how to apply the skill components to develop self-respect and respect for others and how to behave appropriately.

6. *Practice:* The teacher will distribute the worksheet "Road Map" for students to complete as a class assignment and discuss in class.

7. *Independent Use:* The teacher will have students complete the worksheet "Jump Ahead" as a homework assignment and return the assignment in one week for use as the basis for a further class discussion.

8. *Continuation:* The teacher should use classroom opportunities to point out the importance of accepting physical features that cannot be changed and improving personal characteristics in order to develop self-respect and respect for others. He/she will emphasize that improvements of personal characteristics to maintain self-respect must be pursued throughout life.

Name _____ Date _____

ROAD MAP

Directions: Follow the directions below to design your road map to success in the development of self-respect.

START HERE

List five positive features about yourself.

1. _____
2. _____
3. _____
4. _____
5. _____

MOVE AHEAD

List one physical feature about yourself that you dislike but will learn to "live with."

1. _____

Tell how you will accomplish this.

1. _____
2. _____
3. _____

MOVE FURTHER

List three personal features about yourself that you would like to improve.

1. _____
2. _____
3. _____

List one thing you will do to achieve each of the improvements you have listed above.

1. _____
2. _____
3. _____

KEEP MOVING FORWARD

SUCCESS YOU ARE HERE!

Name _____ Date _____

JUMP AHEAD

Directions: Janice has been pressured by her friends to join the gang. As part of the initiation, she has to be "jumped in" (beaten) by the gang members. Next to numbers 1–3 on the rope below, list reasons why Janice would be disrespecting herself if she participated in the initiation. Next to numbers 4–6, list positive actions Janice can take to jump ahead to improve herself and maintain self-respect.

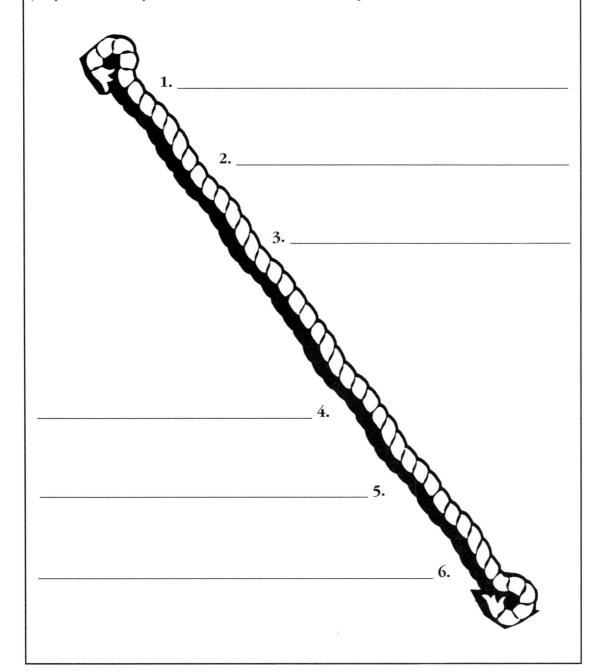

1. _____

2. _____

3. _____

_____ 4.

_____ 5.

_____ 6.

Dealing with Disrespect

Behavioral Objective: Students will learn how to react to a disrespectful situation in a positive manner and maintain an acceptable level of self-respect.

Directed Lesson:

1. **Establish the Need:** Students sometimes use violence as a tool for responding to persons who they feel are disrespectful. To disrespect, or to "dis" in street terms, can easily lead to an assault, fight, stabbing, or even a shooting. Students must learn to be able to respond to disrespectful remarks in a constructive, non-violent manner.

2. **Introduction:** The teacher asks students to relate a recent television show, or movie, or newspaper article in which violence was used in response to someone being disrespectful. If there is no response, the teacher will tell such a story.

   The teacher then discusses the following questions with students:

   ❱ **What was done to embarrass the person?**
   ❱ **What behaviors would you interpret as being disrespectful?**
   ❱ **How did the person respond to the embarrassment?**
   ❱ **What are the consequences of a violent response to a disrespectful person?**
   ❱ **How would you handle an embarrassing situation?**

3. **Identify the Skill Components:** List the following skill components on the board or on sentence strips:

   1. Define disrespect.
   2. Identify what you feel is disrespectful to you.
   3. Identify the situation which brought about the disrespectful remarks.
   4. Decide upon the best response.
   5. Decide if you should ignore the situation.
   6. Decide what you can do to minimize the embarrassing effect on you.
   7. Decide how you can "save face."
   8. Do what you have decided upon.

4. **Model the Skill:** The teacher will share a situation involving disrespect that he/she experienced and explain how to handle the situation in an appropriate manner, such as:

The teacher falls when going up a set of stairs in school, while hurrying to class. Students begin to laugh . . . . The teacher makes a comment, "I guess I'm real clumsy" . . . calls to a student to give him/her "a hand" . . . continues on her/his way to class.

5. *Behavioral Rehearsal:*

   A. *Selection:* The teacher will ask several pairs of students to relate a personal situation where someone showed disrespect to them in front of others and they will respond in a non-violent way using the skill components.

   B. *Role Play:* Each pair of students will be given five minutes to prepare their role play to enact the situation involving disrespect. Each of the three pairs of students will enact their situation, explaining their peaceful responses afterwards and how these responses were derived by following the skill components.

   C. *Completion:* After each role play, the teacher should reinforce the correct behavior and identify inappropriate behaviors. The students should repeat the role play with corrections. If it was well done and correct, the role play is complete.

   D. *Reinforcers:* The class should applaud all role plays. Verbal and nonverbal praise from both the teacher and the class is essential.

   E. *Discussion:* The teacher will encourage other class members to share similar situations they experienced and to ask questions about what difficulties they had using the skill components.

6. **Practice:** Distribute copies of the worksheet "Dealin' with Dissin'" for students to complete in class. When they are ready, discuss their response to each situation described in the worksheet.

7. **Independent Use:** Ask students to complete the worksheet entitled "Step Back, Not Attack" at home. They are to interview three of their friends who responded to a disrespectful situation in a non-violent way and describe how the situation was handled. The worksheet should be completed in one week (or other given period) and returned for use in class discussion.

8. **Continuation:** The teacher will indicate that disrespectful situations occur throughout one's school experience as well as in later life, and will take time to make sure that students apply the skill components when such situations occur. He/she will reemphasize the use of the skill components when these situations arise and suggest a reference to this lesson.

Name _____ Date _____

DEALIN' WITH DISSIN'

Directions: For each embarrassing situation below, explain what you would *feel* like doing and then what you *should* do using the skill components.

1. You are walking into the building at the start of school. As you start up the stairs, someone accidentally bumps into you. You fall down and your books drop to the ground. Everybody, including your friends you are walking with, laughs.

   a. What might you *feel* like doing?

   b. What *should* you do? (Use the skill components.)

2. You are walking with some friends in the lunchroom. A "bully" who has been harassing you walks past and says, "What are you looking at, punk?" All of your friends and others at the nearby lunch tables get quiet and look to you as the "bully" continues walking on.

   a. What might you *feel* like doing?

   b. What *should* you do? (Use the skill components.)

Name _____ Date _____

STEP BACK, NOT ATTACK

Directions: Interview three of your friends outside of this class. Ask them to tell you about a situation in which they were embarrassed or treated disrespectfully in front of others and handled themselves in a manner similar to that in the skill components. These situations should be ones where instead of attacking (responding in a violent manner) they stepped back and acted in a non-violent manner. Without using names, summarize below each situation and how each person responded appropriately.

Friend 1:

Friend 2:

Friend 3:

Developing Communication Skills

Behavioral Objective: Students will develop skills to make friends and to share their feelings, so that they will be able to relieve stress through communicating with others.

Directed Lesson:

1. Establish the Need: Unresolved stress may often lead to more serious consequences, including suicide. Open, accurate, and honest communications with others can provide an avenue to relieve stress, solve a myriad of problems among teenagers, and reduce serious difficulties before they become major events.

2. Introduction: The teacher will read the following story to the class:

> **Sarah is an eleventh grade student at Mercy High School. She had a rewarding childhood and has been given many freedoms by her parents. She came to Mercy from a smaller parochial school where she had many close friends. These friends were so close that each knew the others well. They had especially good peer relationships.**
>
> **Being a new eleventh grader, Sarah made a few new friends but felt somewhat lonely. Many of the students saw Sarah as a "new kid on the block" and often did things that in many respects were done to "initiate" her into the group. Each time something occurred, such as a note on her locker that read "Sarah is a nerd," she withdrew further from the school group and gravitated back to her "old" friends at the former high school. She was always hesitant to discuss the situation that concerned her with the few friends she has made at the new school.**

The teacher asks:

- ▶ **Should Sarah seek new friends? Why?**
- ▶ **How should she communicate her feelings to her closest friends at the new school?**
- ▶ **How can she build a larger group of friends?**
- ▶ **Should she rely on support in these new situations from her former school friends? Why? or Why not? (List on the board.)**

3. Identify the Skill Components: List the following skill components on the board.

1. Assess your strengths and weaknesses.

2. Undertake actions that demonstrate your strengths.

3. Confide and/or seek advice from others.

4. Give praise to others.

5. Resist fear of new situations.

6. Communicate about yourself.

7. Discuss your weaknesses.

8. Show interest in the problems of others.

9. Join in discussions when you are knowledgeable.

10. Develop interest in specific subjects.

4. *Model the Skill:* The teacher will model with a student how to start a relationship and create a friendship by using the skill components.

5. *Behavioral Rehearsal:*

A. *Selection:* The teacher will select five pairs of students.

B. *Role Play:* The teacher will ask each pair of students to demonstrate how they communicate with each other. One student will be asked to try to interest the other one in becoming his/her friend. The students will use their own best ideas together with the skill components. The teacher might ask one student, of several pairs of students, to role play Sarah's part from the story in the introduction.

C. *Completion:* After the role play, the teacher will highlight the best responses, correct inappropriate behavior, and have students redo the role play if necessary. If there are no corrections, the role play is complete.

D. *Reinforcers:* The teacher and peers will thank students for sharing role plays and for appropriately completing the role play using the skill components. The class will identify the best role play and provide special compliments/recognition to the participants for their efforts.

E. *Discussion:* The teacher will lead a class discussion of the different feelings, opinions, and behaviors each student involved in the role plays had made in order to gain a friend and how the "friend" reacted.

6. *Practice:* Hand out copies of the worksheet "Who Am I?" and have students complete and discuss the worksheet in class.

7. *Independent Use:* Distribute copies of the worksheet "Name Your Bandages" for students to complete at home. Ask them to return the finished worksheet in one week to discuss in class.

8. *Continuation:* Throughout the year, the teacher will reinforce the importance of expressing feelings and concerns to others who are recognized as being friends and confidants and to enlist their support.

Name _____ Date _____

WHO AM I?

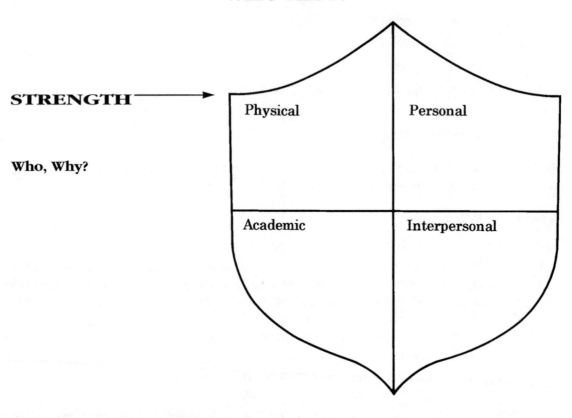

STRENGTH →

Who, Why?

Physical | Personal

Academic | Interpersonal

Physical | Personal

Academic | Interpersonal

← **WEAKNESS**

Who, Why?

Directions: Complete each "Who Am I?" shield. Then indicate those in your "circle of friends" whom you could confide in to either BETTER OR LESSEN those traits you have listed in your shields. Also, draw 2 caricatures in each quadrant of each shield to portray the characteristics you have listed. (The shields may be enlarged.)

Name _____ Date _____

NAME YOUR BANDAGES

This is all about:

Identifying people in your life who can give you help and support when you have problems. Whom can you communicate with?

What you will do:

We all have times in our lives when we feel cut, hurt, and scraped. Just as you use real bandages as aids when you are physically hurt, you have people you know who will act as bandages or band-aids when you are emotionally hurt.

1. Describe the seven situations below and identify whom you would turn to to be a "bandage" in each situation, and why.

2. Write a letter to your favorite "bandage" telling why you value that person in your life.

Situation	**"Bandage" or "Band-Aid"**
1. Rejection	Who Why
2. Poor grades	Who Why
3. Fight with your best friend	Who Why
4. Did not make the team	Who Why
5. Friend with a problem	Who Why
6. Family problems	Who Why
7. Illness	Who Why

Establishing a Good Relationship

Behavioral Objective: The students will learn to nurture a good relationship which provides respect, care, and understanding and to avoid a relationship which brings with it possessiveness, jealousy, pressure to have sex, and unwanted pregnancy.

Directed Lessons:

1. **Establish the Need:** Young people from dysfunctional homes are frequently neglected and even mistreated. Therefore, they yearn for love and companionship. Since these youngsters do not get care, love, and attention at home, they often seek love and attention outside the home, frequently in a relationship with someone of the opposite sex. Seeking love for the only purpose of filling a void can result in unhealthy relationships with possessiveness, jealousy, violence, pressure to have sex, and unwanted pregnancy.

2. **Introduction:** The teacher will pose the following question, then lead the class in response:

   What would you think is a good relationship between two young people of your age? Let us answer this question by listing the desired behaviors and attitudes on the left side of the board and the undesirable behaviors and attitudes on the right side.

   The teacher will start with two behaviors and then get more from the class. The two behaviors are jealousy and respect. The teacher will ask the class on which side the two behaviors belong. The teacher then asks the students to name more behaviors and tell on which side they belong.

   The teacher then reads the following scenario:

   I'd like to tell you about Monique and Travis. Monique is 15 and she lives in a violent home. Although she is very attractive and a good student, her parents seldom give her praise or show any affection towards her. Travis, age 16, is her first boyfriend. They have been going steady for three months. They have some really great times together. It seems that Travis always knows the right thing to say or do to make Monique feel good. Everyone says they are an ideal couple. Their relationship can go two ways. How do you think it will go?

3. **Identify the Skill Components:** List the following skill components on the board:

   1. Analyze your relationship at home.
   2. Decide if you yearn for a good relationship.
   3. Define the meaning of a good relationship.

4. Define the behaviors you desire.

5. Define the behaviors you dislike.

6. Define the responsibilities each of you has.

7. Nurture such a relationship.

8. Show mutual respect, understanding, and care.

9. Enjoy the relationship.

4. ***Model the Skill:*** The teacher will share a scenario from his/her experience and use the skill components to show the steps he/she would go through to inject into the relationship the love and attention needed and to avoid unwanted abuse. The teacher will role play such a scenario by her/himself or designate a student to play act the part of a friend.

5. ***Behavioral Rehearsal:***

   A. *Selection:* Select two pairs of students, preferably one boy and one girl each, to role play the script in the introduction.

   B. *Role Play:* Each pair of students will role play the two characters of the story in the introduction. In one role play, Monique will demonstrate the skills necessary to avoid an unwanted pregnancy. In the second role play, respect for each other might be modeled with special emphasis on the responsibility each of them has.

   C. *Completion:* Following the role play the teacher will reinforce correct behaviors, identify inappropriate behaviors, and have students re-enact role play with corrections. When role play is done correctly, it is complete.

   D. *Reinforcers:* The teacher will congratulate the actors for an understanding and real-life performance. The class will give verbal praise on how well Monique resolved the matter and how well everyone did in the role plays.

   E. *Discussion:* The teacher will begin the discussion by asking questions such as:

   ◗ **How does a young person feel when she/he does not receive affection from family members?**

   ◗ **Can you receive the same type of love from a relationship with a friend that you expect from family members?**

   ◗ **Why did Monique think she was in love with Travis?**

   ◗ **What are some of the lines fellows use to try and get girls to have sex with them?**

   ◗ **What are some of the lines girls can use to say no?**

   ◗ **How should a girl behave on a date? How should a boy behave on a date?**

   ◗ **How does the girl's demeanor influence the fellow's behavior?**

6. ***Practice:*** Distribute copies of the worksheet "Relationships" for students to complete and discuss in class.

7. ***Independent Use:*** Ask the students to interview family, friends, teens, strangers, etc., close to their own age, about their relationships with others. Using these interviews, stu-

dents are to judge which relationships are good ones and report about them. (No names should be mentioned.) They should also report the numbers of interviews they had, how many they judged were good relationships, and what to look out for in order not to be trapped into an abusive relationship. Ask students to complete and submit their reports within a week for class discussion.

8. ***Continuation:*** The teacher will emphasize the beauty of a good relationship and the negative consequences of unstable relationships and point out the importance of choosing partners carefully not only during the teen years, but in adult years also; not only with members of the opposite sex but also with those of the same gender.

Name _____ Date _____

RELATIONSHIPS

Directions: Write brief definitions of each of the behaviors listed in the boxes below. Then, in the space underneath or on the back of the page, write a paragraph or more stating why certain behaviors describe a good and stable relationship while other behaviors are unwanted and a warning signal for not starting a relationship.

Stable Relationship

Behaviors	*Definition*
Respect	
Communications	
Compromise	
Love	
Care	
Attention	
Pleasure	

Unstable Relationship

Behaviors	*Definition*
Jealousy	
Possessiveness	
Violence/Crime	
Coercion	
Neglect	

Resolving Conflicts Peacefully

Behavioral Objective: Students will learn to resolve conflicts peacefully and in a way so that each person feels satisfied with the solution.

Directed Lesson:

1. ***Establish the Need:*** Disagreements between people, even if of minor importance, frequently lead to hot tempers and angry reactions which can result in fights and other violent responses. When weapons are available, violence can lead to death. Students need to learn non-violent ways to express and release their anger and to develop skills which will allow them to resolve conflicts in a peaceful manner. The skills of this lesson, based on conflict resolution methods, will help students to do just this.

2. ***Introduction:*** The teacher will read the following story:

   It was Monday morning. Sara didn't want to get up and go to school. She was tired, her bed felt so nice and warm, plus, it was snowing outside. As Sara started to get out of bed, she noticed that her new puppy had had an "accident" in her sneakers and was now chewing on her favorite sweater. She yelled at the puppy and flung a pillow at him. The puppy hid under the bed.

   Sara got up, showered, brushed her teeth, did her hair and finally went down to breakfast still feeling mad about her shoes and favorite sweater, which was now a big ball of yarn. Why did she have to go to school? Why couldn't it be Saturday, she thought.

   After eating breakfast, Sara got her backpack and headed for the bus stop. When she arrived, some of the boys were throwing snowballs at a snowman someone had made next to the sidewalk at the bus stop. As Sara was bending over to check for her homework in her backpack, a large snowball landed very near her splattering her with snow. "Hey," she yelled, "Who did that?" Mark admitted that he had thrown the snowball but added, "I didn't mean for it to hit you." By this time some of the others waiting for the bus began to laugh. This really made Sara mad. "Oh, yes you did, you dummy! See how *you* like it!" and with that she packed a large snowball and threw it directly at Mark's face. Her aim was good and Mark got a face full of snow. Mark yelled, "That's not fair. My snowball hit you by accident, but you did it on purpose." Then Mark threw a snowball at Sara hitting her on the side of her head. Next, the two were fighting.

   The teacher will ask students the following questions:

   ▶ **Why did Sara and Mark really get into a fight?**

> **What was at the root of Sara's anger?**

> **How could the fight have been avoided?**

> **Was there something that Mark or someone else could have said or done that would have helped bring about a more peaceful solution?**

3. ***Identify the Skill Components:*** Write the following skill components on the board:

1. Step back from the situation and "cool off."

2. Decide how the conflict started.

3. Try to understand each person's point of view.

4. Listen to what others are saying.

5. Establish each person's responsibility.

6. Consider possible solutions.

7. Choose a peaceful solution.

8. Commit to upholding the solution.

9. Thank all parties for their involvement in arriving at a peaceful solution.

4. ***Model the Skill:*** The teacher will model the skill by using a conflict from his/her personal experience. He/she will use the skill components to show how the conflict selected can be peacefully resolved.

5. ***Behavioral Rehearsal:***

    A. *Selection:* The teacher will select 3 groups of two students each.

    B. *Role Play:* The teacher will have the following conflict-producing situations on index cards. Each pair of students will be given an index card and will role play the following situations.

    – Tony is in a long line to buy tickets to the baseball game. Phil cuts in front of Tony; a fight is about to begin.

    – Candice spills Janet's milk all over Janet's sandwich, by accident.

    – Stephanie sees Sharon smoking cigarettes and tells the teacher, who gives Sharon a lecture about not smoking. Sharon sees Stephanie standing with some friends after school. As Sharon approaches, she asks Stephanie if she was the one who told the teacher she was smoking.

    C. *Completion:* The teacher and other students will decide if the role plays were correct and if the skill components were applied appropriately in the role plays. If not, they will identify the incorrect behaviors and reenact the role plays with corrections. If there are no corrections, role play is complete.

    D. *Reinforcers:* The teacher and class will thank the participants for their participation with applause or any other form of positive reinforcement.

    E. *Discussion:* The teacher will ask: **How can a small disagreement or accidental action result in a serious confrontation or fight, even death?** The teacher will have students discuss the possible difficulties they might encounter while trying to come to a peaceful solution. The teacher will ask why it is better to solve a conflict peacefully than to go with "hot" tempers and violent reactions into an argument.

6. ***Practice:*** The teacher will distribute the worksheet entitled "Conflict Strategies" to be completed by students and discussed in class. This worksheet will tell the students about themselves and their behavioral traits which they will share and discuss with their classmates.

   When students have completed the worksheet, hand out copies of the "Conflict Strategies Tally Sheet" and ask them to record and total their responses. They can then read the descriptions of the various conflict strategies which follow.

   NOTE: None of these strategies is necessarily better than another. Different strategies are appropriate in different circumstances.

7. ***Independent Use:*** Give students the worksheet "A Conflict In My Life" to complete outside of class and to return within a week, to share in class.

8. ***Continuation:*** The teacher will discuss the importance of using conflict resolution skills to avoid conflicts before they occur or, if they are unavoidable, resolve them in a peaceful manner. He/she will point out that these skills will be helpful throughout their entire lives and that it is never too early or too late to learn these skills and to use them.

Name _____ Date _____

CONFLICT STRATEGIES

Directions: The proverbs listed below can be thought of as descriptions of some of the different strategies for resolving conflicts. Proverbs state traditional wisdom, and these proverbs reflect traditional ways of dealing with conflicts. Carefully, using the following scale, indicate how typical each proverb is of your actions in conflict situations.

5 = very typical of the way I act in a conflict
4 = frequently typical of the way I act in a conflict
3 = sometimes typical of the way I act in a conflict
2 = seldom typical of the way I act in a conflict
1 = never typical of the way I act in a conflict

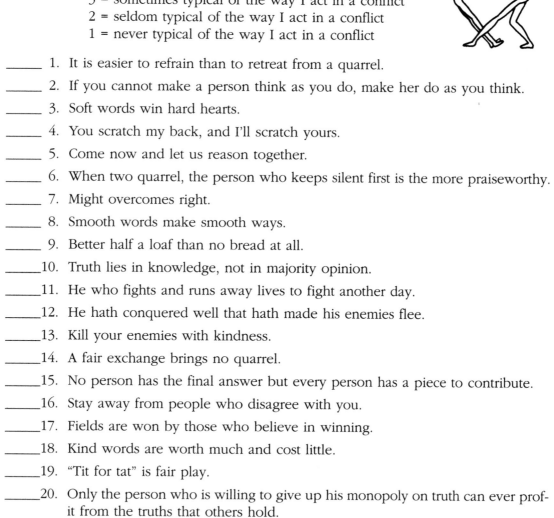

_____ 1. It is easier to refrain than to retreat from a quarrel.

_____ 2. If you cannot make a person think as you do, make her do as you think.

_____ 3. Soft words win hard hearts.

_____ 4. You scratch my back, and I'll scratch yours.

_____ 5. Come now and let us reason together.

_____ 6. When two quarrel, the person who keeps silent first is the more praiseworthy.

_____ 7. Might overcomes right.

_____ 8. Smooth words make smooth ways.

_____ 9. Better half a loaf than no bread at all.

_____10. Truth lies in knowledge, not in majority opinion.

_____11. He who fights and runs away lives to fight another day.

_____12. He hath conquered well that hath made his enemies flee.

_____13. Kill your enemies with kindness.

_____14. A fair exchange brings no quarrel.

_____15. No person has the final answer but every person has a piece to contribute.

_____16. Stay away from people who disagree with you.

_____17. Fields are won by those who believe in winning.

_____18. Kind words are worth much and cost little.

_____19. "Tit for tat" is fair play.

_____20. Only the person who is willing to give up his monopoly on truth can ever profit from the truths that others hold.

_____21. Avoid quarrelsome people as they will only make your life miserable.

_____22. A person who will not flee will make others flee.

_____23. Soft words ensure harmony.

_____24. One gift for another makes good friends.

Conflict Strategies *(cont'd)*

_____25. Bring your conflicts into the open and face them directly; only then will the best solution be discovered.

_____26. The best way of handling conflicts is to avoid them.

_____27. Put your foot down where you mean to stand.

_____28. Gentleness will triumph over anger.

_____29. Getting part of what you want is better than not getting anything at all.

_____30. Frankness, honesty, and trust will move mountains.

_____31. There is nothing so important you have to fight for it.

_____32. There are two kinds of people in the world, the winners and the losers.

_____33. When someone hits you with a stone, hit him with a piece of cotton.

_____34. When both give in halfway, a fair settlement is achieved.

_____35. By digging and digging, the truth is discovered.

Name _____ Date _____

CONFLICT STRATEGIES TALLY SHEET

Directions: Record the number you have given for each item on the Conflict Strategies worksheet below and total each column. Then read the description of each strategy which follows:

Withdrawing turtle	Forcing shark	Smoothing teddy bear	Compromising fox	Confronting owl
____1	____2	____3	____4	____5
____6	____7	____8	____9	____10
____11	____12	____13	____14	____15
____16	____17	____18	____19	____20
____21	____22	____23	____24	____25
____26	____27	____28	____29	____30
____31	____32	____33	____34	____35
TOTAL:____	TOTAL:____	TOTAL:____	TOTAL:____	TOTAL:____

Description of conflict strategies:

Turtles withdraw to avoid conflicts
give up personal goals and relationships
stay away from controversial issues
believe managing conflicts is hopeless
feel helpless

Sharks overpower opponents by attacking and intimidating
refuse to abandon their goals under any circumstance
do not value personal relationships
are not influenced by the need to be liked
believe conflicts are solved by winning and losing
feel proud in winning and inadequacy in losing

Teddy Bears think relationships are very important
consider their goals of little importance
want to be liked and accepted
value harmony
believe conflict damages relationships
will give up goals to preserve a relationship

Foxes are moderately concerned about their goals and personal relationships
seek compromise
are willing to give up their goals and persuade others to also
look for middle ground and agreement to solve conflicts

Owls value their own goals highly
consider relationships to be very important
view conflicts as problems to be solved
believe that conflict can improve relationships
seek to satisfy the needs and goals of all parties
need tensions and negative feelings to be completely resolved

None of these is necessarily better than another. Different strategies are appropriate in different circumstances. If you use one exclusively, that can be a problem.

Name _____ Date _____

A CONFLICT IN MY LIFE
My Side vs. the Other Side

Directions: Think of a recent situation which involved a conflict between you and a parent, brother/sister, or friend. Describe the facts of the conflict situation in the form of a newspaper headline which clearly explains the conflict and the solution. Use the skill components.

The Conflict   _____

                                _____

My Side   _____

The Other Side   _____

Solutions   _____

                                _____

                                _____

                                _____

                                _____

The Solution   _____
How I Feel Now,
Looking Back   _____

What I Have Learned   _____
in This Lesson
                                _____

                                _____

                                _____

                                _____

                                _____

                                _____

Accepting Responsibilities When Exercising Rights

Behavioral Objective: Students will learn that their individual rights as citizens can be exercised only when they are willing to assume responsibility and accountability for their actions.

Directed Lesson:

l. **Establish the Need:** Young people are often quick to claim what they believe are their rights, but at the same time they often fail to recognize their responsibilities. They overemphasize their rights without the desire to recognize their responsibilities. They will frequently say or think "Society owes me this or that" as an excuse for their unlawful actions, such as theft, robbery, drug sales, or other offenses. So, young people will have to recognize that they will only be able to have what is rightfully theirs and then only if they accept the responsibility for their own actions, which means that they will have to stay within the boundaries of what is considered to be the law of this country. They have to realize that they must contribute as well as receive.

2. **Introduction:** The teacher will discuss the following questions with the class:

   ▶ **What rights do we have as teachers and school employees?**

   ▶ **What responsibilities do we have as teachers and school employees?**

   ▶ **What rights do your parents/family members have in society?**

   ▶ **What responsibilities do your parents/family members have in society?**

   ▶ **What rights do you have as citizens?**

   ▶ **What responsibilities do you have as citizens?**

3. **Identify the Skill Components:** List the following skill components on the board or on sentence strips:

   1. Identify your rights as a member of society.

   2. Identify rights you do not have.

   3. Uphold the rights of others.

   4. Identify your responsibilities to society.

   5. Decide how to show your accountability.

   6. Plan to exercise your responsibility.

   7. Do as planned.

4. ***Model the Skill:*** The teacher will give an example of how he/she has the right to express an opinion, but at the same time has the responsibility to express it in such a way so as not to offend or hurt the other person. The teacher will use the skill components to do this.

5. ***Behavioral Rehearsal:***

   A. *Selection:* The teacher will select four pairs of students and give each pair an index card with a right printed on one side and a corresponding responsibility printed on the other side. Each pair of students will discuss how to honor both the right and the responsibility.

   B. *Role Play:* The teacher will prepare four index cards with rights and related responsibilities for each pair of students to role play.

   The following rights and responsibilities may be considered:

   – The right to go to college. The responsibility to study hard and make good grades.

   – The right to do a job. The responsibility to do the job well.

   – The right to earn a driver's license. The responsibility to learn and abide by the laws of the road.

   – The right to go out for a sport. The responsibility to maintain good grades in order to participate.

   C. *Completion:* The teacher and peers will analyze the role play and the use of the skill components and have students re-enact the role play if corrections are necessary. If no corrections are needed, the role play is complete.

   D. *Reinforcers:* The teacher and students will compliment the role players for their performance.

   E. *Discussion:* The teacher and class will list appropriate rights and responsibilities on the board and participate in a class discussion of how to use the skill components to enable the students to exercise their rights and at the same time accept their responsibilities.

6. ***Practice:*** The teacher will divide the class into three or more groups and hand out a copy of the worksheet "Rights and Responsibilities" to each group. Direct each group to identify two rights they have as students, two rights they have as citizens, and a corresponding responsibility for each of the rights. When all groups have completed the worksheet, the class will discuss the results of each group.

7. ***Independent Use:*** The teacher will distribute copies of the worksheet "Which Right Is Right?" for students to take home and complete and ask them to return their completed worksheets for a class discussion the following week.

8. ***Continuation:*** The teacher will continue to identify the responsibilities of youth as students and citizens throughout the school year, emphasizing that rights can be exercised only if they do not interfere with the rights of others and if responsibilities are accepted to safeguard the rights of others.

Name _____ Date _____

RIGHTS AND RESPONSIBILITIES

Directions: List two rights you have as a student, two rights you have as a citizen, and a responsibility that is related to each right.

RIGHT   RESPONSIBILITY

As a student:

1. _____   1. _____

2. _____   2. _____

As a citizen:

1. _____   1. _____

2. _____   2. _____

Name _____ Date _____

WHICH RIGHT IS RIGHT?

Directions: Think about a right you have that is important to you. Then think about a right of another person that conflicts with your right(s), such as their right to freedom of speech vs. your right to education.

1. State a right that is important to you.

2. State a right which conflicts with your right, but is important to another person.

3. Explain how the two rights conflict.

4. Explain the responsibilities that each person has when exercising these rights.

5. Explain how each person can make sure that the rights of the other person are respected.

RELATIONSHIPS Lesson 11

Understanding the Importance of Being Selective in Choosing Friends

Behavioral Objective: Students will learn the importance of being selective in choosing friends and to realize that this will make it easier for them to stay away from illegal activities such as indulging in stimulants, stealing, etc.

1. ***Establish the Need:*** Students know that peers can have a very powerful influence on what activities they join and on their likes and dislikes. They thus need to understand that choosing the right friends is most important for preserving appropriate behavior since the right friends will make it easy for them to stay away from illegal activities, such as joining groups which indulge in stimulants, sex orgies, shootouts, and so on. By informing themselves about the activities of their peers, young people will be better able to judge whom to befriend and join in recreational activities.

2. ***Introduction:*** The teacher will read the following story to the class:

   Tamera and Kinesha were invited to a party. They were both excited about being invited and thought of it as being their chance to hang with the in-crowd.

   Upon arriving at the party, they checked out the scene. There were a lot of students from their school and also a lot of people they had never seen before. The music was great and a lot of people were dancing and just having fun.

   As they walked around from one room to the next, they noticed many people drinking or using drugs. They both began to feel uncomfortable. It was during this time that a girl named Matilda came up to the girls and asked them if they wanted to meet some boys.

   Although Matilda went to the same school as Tamera and Kinesha, the two girls did not know her very well. They noticed that Matilda had been drinking and smoking pot, and that she didn't seem to be making any sense at times. She introduced them to three guys that they had never seen before.

   After talking for a while, the guys started asking Tamera and Kinesha to join them in smoking a joint. The girls kept saying, "No thanks," but the guys kept pressuring them. Then the guys tried to put their arms around the girls and kiss them. That's when Tamera and Kinesha decided that it was time to leave the party. Matilda was not ready to leave. She wanted to stay and party some more. She could not say "no" to her friends that were pressuring her.

   A few days later, Tamera and Kinesha saw Matilda at school. She didn't remember talking to them at the party, and wished she had left with them. Matilda had gotten into a fight at the party.

One of the guy's girlfriends showed up at the party and approached Matilda, calling her a slut and then pushing her. A fight started that resulted in Matilda getting a tooth knocked out of her mouth, as well as getting many scratches and marks on her face. Besides the physical injuries, Matilda was really down on herself. Tamera and Kinesha convinced her to talk to the school counselor to help her with her problems.

After a few weeks, Matilda became good friends with Tamera and Kinesha. They started going everywhere together. With the help of her new friends and the guidance counselor, Matilda stayed away from drugs. This gave her enough confidence to say "no"!

The teacher asks the class: **What positive role did the friendship of Tamera and Kinesha play in Matilda's life so that she was able to resist peer pressure and thus remain drug free?**

3. *Identify the Skill Components:* Write the following on the board or on a transparency to be used with an overhead projector, or on sentence strips.

1. Evaluate the situation.
2. Determine if peer pressure made you join.
3. Analyze the gain as a participant.
4. Analyze the consequences.
5. Consider your peers' actions.
6. Consider your options.
7. Reconsider your friendships.
8. Choose the right friends.

4. *Model the Skill:* The teacher will model how a friend helped her/him out of a situation and will use the skill components.

5. *Behavioral Rehearsal:*

   A. *Selection:* The teacher will choose several small groups for role playing. (The number will depend on the time available for the exercise.)

   B. *Role Play:* The groups will role play different situations, such as:

   – Students are at someone's house/or walking to school when someone pulls out a bag of marijuana from his/her pocket and suggests to the others that they smoke some "weed."

   – Students are discussing what they are going to do tonight—go to a dance, movie, ball game, or go to a party where they know there will be drinking and drugs.

   – Students are in a group, when one of the students begins to show how much money, jewelry, and new shoes she/he got by selling drugs, and tries to recruit others to help to sell drugs.

C. *Completion:* After each role play, the teacher will reinforce correct behaviors, identify inappropriate behaviors, and ask students to reenact role play with corrections. If there are no corrections, role play is complete.

D. *Reinforcers:* The teacher and peers will give verbal and non-verbal praise (specific) for correct role plays.

E. *Discussion:* When the role plays are concluded, the teacher will start a discussion by asking the following questions:

- **Our role plays today dealt with stimulants and drugs. What other illegal "recreational" activities have serious consequences?**

- **Will a good friendship be helpful in avoiding temptation?**

- **Can peers put an enormous pressure upon you, and any of us?**

- **How can you best counter such pressure?**

6. **Practice:** Distribute copies of the worksheet "Right Friends" for students to complete and discuss in class.

7. **Independent Use:** Ask students to write a short story of at least one page telling how they can be a friend to another person and help to keep him/her from joining groups involved in illegal activities. Ask students to bring their stories to class in one week and to share them with their classmates.

8. **Continuation:** The teacher will emphasize how important it is to choose the right friends not only at school but throughout our entire lives. The right friends cannot only help us overcome difficult situations but also keep us out of experiences that we, by ourselves, might have been tempted to seek.

Name _____ Date _____

"RIGHT" FRIENDS

I. List 4 different situations when a "right" friend helped you to get through a situation. (These situations do not have to be school related.)

1. _____

2. _____

3. _____

4. _____

II. Copy the skill components from the board.

1. _____

2. _____

3. _____

4. _____

5. _____

6. _____

7. _____

8. _____

III. Choose one of the situations you listed at the top of the page. Use the skill components to explain how the friend helped get you through your situation.

_____

_____

_____

_____

_____

_____

_____

Understanding Male/Female Relationships

Behavioral Objective: The students will learn to appreciate and cherish good relationships with partners of the opposite sex by learning to understand that it is most important to respect each other, to commiserate honestly, and to compromise in order to please.

Directed Lessons:

1. ***Establish the Need:*** The phrase "looking for love in all the wrong places" is especially true for young people who come from homes where they feel uncared for, unappreciated, and unloved. In their efforts to find loving, caring relationships, young people often mistake any attention especially from the opposite sex, as what they are looking for and what they feel they deserve. Unscrupulous people of all ages can spot these youngsters and quickly take advantage of them. The young person believes he/she has found someone who truly cares about and loves them; he/she is willing to do anything to keep the relationship going. This vulnerability of the young person can lead to unhealthy and unsafe life styles, such as suffering abuse, being "dropped" by the other person causing great emotional suffering, and in extreme cases involvement in drugs, prostitution, pornography and other crimes. Students need to learn how to find the caring, loving relationships they need with persons of the opposite sex, which will nurture them, not harm them.

2. ***Introduction:*** The teacher will tell the following story about Monique and Travis:

   > **Monique is 15 years old. Although she is attractive and is a good student, her parents seldom show her affection, give praise or spend time with her. They are busy with their careers and fighting with each other. Yesterday at the mall, Monique met Travis, a 19-year-old, who was "window shopping" when Travis started talking to her. He was very nice and polite. After talking for a few minutes, he asked her to go to the food court and have a Coke with him. She did and had a great time. He made her laugh and feel good. He told her how pretty she was and how smart she sounded. He asked her for her phone number so he could call her; she gave it readily. Her mind was racing with thoughts of sweet smiles, affectionate hugs and kisses, going places together. Later that evening, after Monique was home, Travis called and asked her to meet him at the mall the next day after school. Monique said she would be there.**

   The teacher will ask:

   - **What is the best relationship that could develop between Monique and Travis?**

   - **What could happen if Travis is an unscrupulous person? How could this relationship be unhealthy or unsafe for Monique? What could be the consequences?**

> ▶ **Why is Monique vulnerable?**
>
> ▶ **What are the signs of a healthy/stable relationship? . . . an unhealthy/unstable relationship?**

(List both on board)

3. ***Identify the Skill Components:*** Write the following skill components on the board or on sentence strips:

1. Remember that mutual respect is essential.
2. Consider your motives for the relationship.
3. Consider your partner's motives.
4. Decide your level of comfort in the relationship.
5. Determine if this relationship is healthy/stable or unhealthy/unstable.
6. Think about the long-term consequences of the relationship.
7. If healthy/stable, continue to work to make it better.
8. If unhealthy/unstable, leave the relationship.
9. Make the decision sooner rather than later.

4. ***Model the Skill:*** The teacher will share a relationship situation of his/her own choice and demonstrate the use of the skill components to help the relationship to grow or to end if necessary in order to avoid unwanted consequences.

5. ***Behavioral Rehearsal:***

   A. *Selection:* The teacher will select the needed number of students for the role plays.

   B. *Role Play:* The teacher will ask the students to develop their own role play based on the subject matter or to use the following role plays.

   – Jim and Dolly have been dating for three months. They have started having sex because Dolly said she would quit dating Jim if he didn't have sex with her. Now Jim is worried that Dolly will get pregnant and insist on getting married. He has been using "protection" but accidents do happen. This would ruin his plans to go to college.

   – Kim has been dating Gordon for about a year. He says he loves her but he never wants to do anything she suggests. He jokes with his friends in front of her about her weight and he has begun to slap her when he gets angry about something.

   C. *Completion:* The teacher and students will determine if the skill components were used in the role plays and if the role plays were correct. If not, the role plays should be re-played with corrections. The role play is complete if there are no corrections.

   D. *Reinforcers:* The role players' efforts should be acknowledged verbally, with applause, or in other ways, with special praise given to the best role play.

   E. *Discussion:* The teacher will encourage discussion by asking the following questions:

▶ **How could your life at home influence the relationship you have with a person of the opposite sex?**

▶ **What are some of the "lines" an uncaring person could use to begin and maintain a relationship with a young person (girl or boy)?**

▶ **What made Jim feel uncomfortable in the first role play? Was his worry valid?**

▶ **What were the "pros" and "cons" of the relationship in the second role play?**

(List these on the board.)

▶ **What will be the long-term effect of this relationship?**

6. ***Practice:*** The teacher will distribute copies of the worksheet "Relationships" for students to complete in class and discuss the finished papers.

7. ***Independent Use:*** The teacher will hand out the worksheet "Relationship Interviews" for the students to complete at home and return in one week to discuss in class.

8. ***Continuation:*** The teacher will emphasize the beauty of a good, healthy, stable relationship and the negative consequences of a bad, unhealthy and unstable relationship. Students should be encouraged to carefully choose partners not only for dating but also for life-long friendships. The teacher will also explain that relationships can help boost the feeling of being appreciated, loved, and admired, such as girl-friend (or boy-friend) relationships, cooperative relationships on the job, and teamwork in athletics.

Name _____ Date _____

RELATIONSHIPS

Directions: Describe each type of relationship by giving examples of the listed behaviors. You can add some behaviors, too.

Healthy/Stable

Behaviors	*Examples*
Respect	
Compromise	
Communication	

Unhealthy/Unstable

Behaviors	*Examples*
Possessiveness	
Coercion	
Jealousy	
Violence	

On the back of this page or below, describe how the skill components could be used to avoid the possible consequences of an unhealthy/unstable relationship.

Name _____ Date _____

RELATIONSHIP INTERVIEWS

Directions: Use this form to interview three adult family members and/or adult friends of the family.

	Indicate Family or Friends	Age Range: 21-31, 31-45, 45-60, over 60	Would you describe this relationship as healthy/stable or unhealthy/unstable?	What positive behaviors were present in the relationship? Describe.	Were there any behaviors that made you feel uncomfortable or feeling bad? Describe.	How did you deal with behaviors that made you feel bad or uncomfortable?
1.						
2.						
3.						

Understanding What "Triggers" Cause Anger

Behavioral Objective: Students will learn that certain words, phrases and actions are triggers that can cause anger and that people are sensitive to different triggers depending on language, culture, nationality, gender, ethnic origin, and so on, and can learn to recognize and control their reactions to these triggers.

Directed Lesson:

1. **Establish the Need:** Teens (and adults) sometimes explode in anger when they hear certain words or see certain actions (like hand signals) which for them trigger their immediate anger. Since these words, behaviors and/or actions cause instant anger, they are called "triggers." Each person, depending on his/her sensitivity, will react with anger in varying degrees, to different triggers. Some triggers are common to a particular culture, gender, etc. In today's mobile, multicultural society, it is especially important for all people not only to recognize triggers to which one's self will react with anger, but also to recognize the triggers of others in order to prevent causing unnecessary anger.

2. **Introduction:** The teacher will ask for examples of "triggers" that might cause anger in some students while others would not be bothered. (List the triggers on the board.) The teacher will ask why this occurs. The teacher will then read the following story to the class.

   Mr. Jensen has just entered the teacher's lounge when he sees Mrs. Jones and heads straight for her. He starts complaining that she left the science supply cabinet open. Before Mrs. Jones can reply, Mr. Sidley interrupts to say that it was he, not Mrs. Jones, who forgot to close and lock the science supply cabinet. Mr. Jensen slaps Mr. Sidley on the back and says that he understands how that could happen since he knows how busy Mr. Sidley gets. Mr. Jensen then turns back to Mrs. Jones and says, "You should not be teaching science anyway since you're a woman! Women are better suited to teaching home economics, business machines and secretarial courses." Mrs. Jones hearing this gets very angry and is "about to explode."

   The teacher will ask the students to identify the triggers that caused Mrs. Jones' anger and tell what they think Mrs. Jones should do.

3. **Identify the Skill Components:** Write the following skill components on the board or on sentence strips:

   1. Pinpoint the triggers that caused your anger.

   2. Analyze why this has made you angry.

   3. Realize the consequences to impulsive actions.

4. Give yourself time to "cool off."

5. Decide how to release your anger in a non-violent manner.

6. Release your anger.

4. ***Model the Skill:*** The teacher will model Mrs. Jones' actions and retorts to complete the story in the introduction by using the skill components.

5. ***Behavioral Rehearsal:***

A. *Selection:* The teacher will have students form groups of 5–6.

B. *Role Play:* Using the list of "triggers" the students suggested during the introduction, the teacher will assign a "trigger" to each group. The group will plan how to role play different reactions to the trigger. Each group will present their role play for the assigned "trigger."

C. *Completion:* After each role play is presented, the teacher will decide if the role play was done correctly and the skill components were properly applied. If not, the role play will be reenacted with corrections; if there are no corrections, the role play is complete.

D. *Reinforcers:* The teacher will compliment the efforts of each group and encourage applause from the other groups and the rest of the class.

E. *Discussion:* The teacher will encourage discussion by asking the following questions:

> ❭ **Why is it important for individuals to know what "triggers" their anger?**

> ❭ **Do some "triggers" cause more intense anger than others, or is it just that some people react more intensely?**

> ❭ **How difficult is it to control reaction to a "trigger"?**

> ❭ **Are all "triggers" verbal?**

> ❭ **How can the skill components help you to control your reaction to "triggers"?**

6. ***Practice:*** The teacher will distribute copies of the worksheet "Triggers" for the students to complete in class and then have students share their stories as time permits.

7. ***Independent Use:*** The teacher will ask each student to design at home a slogan and a poster for themselves to help them "stay cool" or keep control in a "trigger" related situation. Each poster should offer a suggestion to control or diffuse the anger caused by the situation. Posters should be brought to school within the next week to be discussed and displayed around the classroom.

8. ***Continuation:*** The teacher will emphasize that verbal and non-verbal expressions which "trigger" anger will occur throughout our lives. For this reason, it is important for each of us to know how to release our anger by using methods to prevent the anger from getting so intense that it could lead to violence.

Name _____ Date _____

TRIGGERS

Directions: Write a paragraph or two describing an actual or made-up incident in which someone "triggered" your anger by what they said or did. Explain what was said or done, how it made you feel, and how you could react in a controlled or non-violent way with the help of the skill components.

ANGER Lesson 14

Managing Anger

Behavioral Objective: Students will learn that although anger is a normal emotion, they can express their anger in a controlled manner so that they can release the anger without verbal or physical violence.

Directed Lessons:

1. **Establish the Need:** Any person, teenagers as well as adults, will become angry at times because of their reaction to another person's verbal and/or physical expression or because they find themselves in a hopeless, fearful, or embarrassing situation which is self-created or caused by others. It is critical to a person's health and well-being to be able to express anger as long as it can be done in a way which does not increase the anger and the probability of violence. Techniques, such as a "cool off" method, should be used before anyone confronts the responsible person and tries to solve the situation which had caused the anger.

2. **Introduction:** The teacher will explain to the students that a person can deal with anger in a healthy manner which allows the individual to grow as a person and to find creative solutions to problems; or the person can deal with anger in an unhealthy manner which often leads to violence against him/herself or others. As the teacher talks about these two ways of expressing anger, he/she can ask students to give examples of each and list them on the board under the headings "Healthy" and "Unhealthy." Anger can also mask deeper secondary emotions related to rejection, helplessness, fear, embarrassment, sadness, lack of control, and so on.

    The teacher will also point out that as we get angry our bodies usually signal us in various ways that we are becoming angry. The teacher will ask the students to name some "body signals" that occur when we are becoming angry and list them on the board. The teacher will then read the following story:

    > **Susan's four-year-old sister tore many pages out of her history book and then hid the book behind the couch. Since Susan could not find the book to take to class the next day, Susan's teacher scolded her during class and warned her not to come to class unprepared again. When Susan got home from school, she found the book behind the couch and knew who had done this to her book. She started looking through the house for her little sister while yelling "I'm going to kill you."**

    The teacher will ask the students:

    ▶ **What feelings did Susan experience as a result of this situation and why?**

▶ **What do you think could happen to her little sister when she catches her?**

▶ **How could Susan deal with the situation in a non-violent manner?**

3. ***Identify the Skill Components:*** Write the following skill components on the board:

1. Think about what you are feeling.
2. Decide why you are feeling angry.
3. Give yourself time to "cool off."
4. Engage in a non-violent activity to release some of your emotions.
5. Consider the part of the situation over which you have control.
6. Choose a non-violent way to express your anger.
7. Express your anger in a non-violent way.

4. ***Model the Skill:*** The teacher will model the skill using the skill components and the following school-related incident.

On a recent Friday afternoon, a teacher was asked to meet with the principal in his/her office. The principal informed the teacher that the president of the PTA, Mrs. Smith, had called to complain about the "F" grade her daughter had received from the teacher. The principal told the teacher that since Mrs. Smith was the PTA president and very influential the "F" should be changed to a "C." When the teacher refused, the principal stated that the teacher could either change the grade or could look for a new job.

The teacher will ask a student to assist with the modeling by taking the part of the principal with the teacher. The teacher could model the skill alone by "thinking aloud" what the teacher in the story may be feeling and how he/she will deal with these feelings.

5. ***Behavioral Rehearsal:***

A. *Selection:* The teacher will select students to role play, as needed.

B. *Role Play:* The teacher will distribute the following anger-producing situations written on index cards to the role playing students.

 – A student at school called your mother a name.

 – You received a poor grade on your report card.

 – You caught your girlfriend/boyfriend with another person.

 – You heard a nasty rumor about yourself, which was supposed to have been started by your best friend.

 – Several students laughed when you tripped on your untied shoelaces.

 – Again, you were chosen last in a team sport during physical education class.

C. *Completion:* After each role play, the teacher will decide if correct behaviors or incorrect behaviors were used and will ask for re-play if necessary. If there are no corrections, role play is complete.

D. *Reinforcers:* The teacher will acknowledge the role players' participation with "thank you" and applause from the class.

E.   *Discussion:* The teacher will ask the following questions:

> ▶ **Which emotions were part of the angry feelings shown in these role plays?**

> ▶ **What makes it difficult to express your anger in non-violent ways in such situations?**

> ▶ **What are some good reasons for choosing a non-violent expression of anger?**

6. ***Practice:*** The teacher will hand out the worksheet "ANGER" for students to complete and share in class.

7. ***Independent Use:*** The teacher will distribute the worksheet entitled "Angry Situations" for students to complete at home as instructed and to return in one week. At that time in class, discuss the situations and how using the skill components could improve the outcome and achieve a non-violent solution.

8. ***Continuation:*** The teacher will remind students that it can be especially helpful to use the "cool off" steps of the skill components whenever they are in an anger-producing situation which could escalate to violence. The teacher might suggest to the students that they can use this process even when they find themselves in conflicts with their parents. The teacher will emphasize that this skill will be useful throughout their life.

Name _____ Date _____

ANGER

Directions: Complete these sentences:

1. I feel angry when _____
   _____

2. I feel angry when _____
   _____

3. I feel angry when _____
   _____

4. It makes me angry to see/hear _____
   _____

5. It makes me angry to see/hear _____
   _____

6. It makes me angry to see/hear _____
   _____

Choose two statements from above and write a paragraph for each telling how the skill components can help you to express your feelings in an appropriate way. (Use the back of this page if needed.)

Statement number _____.

Statement number _____.

Name _____ Date _____

 ANGRY SITUATIONS

Directions: For the next week, observe family members or others for situations that cause anger. Use this chart to record the interactions and what you might have done in the same situation.

	Person(s)	Describe the situation	Describe how the person(s) reacted.	Describe how you would have reacted using the skill components
M				
T				
W				
TH				
F				
ST				
SN				

Understanding the Futility of Revenge

Behavioral Objective: Students will learn that seeking revenge is futile and does not result in the anticipated outcomes (good feelings, satisfaction, material gain, reduced anger, etc.). Instead, revenge can increase the problem, lead to new problems, cause legal difficulties, and even incarceration and death.

Directed Lesson:

1. **Establish the Need:** Young people sometimes think that when they have been "wronged" in some way, no matter how minor, they must retaliate or seek revenge in order to maintain respect. One act of revenge leads to another and again another and more people are drawn into the conflict, creating volatile and dangerous situations. It is important for young people to understand the negative and harmful consequences of revenge and to learn how to deal with feelings that could result in "seeking to revenge."

2. **Introduction:** The teacher will write the following sentence on the board:

   REVENGE: to inflict harm or injury in return for "a wrong"

   The teacher will then ask students to respond to the following questions:

   - **What causes a person to seek revenge?**
   - **What types of "wrongs" might a person think deserve to be revenged?**
   - **How does a person expect to feel after getting revenge?**
   - **How could "getting revenge" create other problems which could be more serious?**
   - **Does revenge usually end when the "wronged" person retaliates?**
   - **What could be a better way to handle the feelings which cause the wish "to seek revenge"?**

3. **Identify the Skill Components:** Write the following skill components on the board or on sentence strips.

   1. Decide which deed is causing feelings for revenge.
   2. Analyze your feelings of revenge.
   3. Consider the consequences of any acts of revenge.
   4. Think of a solution which will not provoke further need for revenge.
   5. If necessary, discuss with a responsible adult.
   6. Plan a strategy.
   7. Act accordingly.

4. *Model the Skill:* The teacher will use an incident from his/her own past that may have evoked feelings for revenge. After explaining the incident in detail, the teacher will use the skill components to plan how to react. If the teacher has no such incident, he/she can use the following:

> **On Saturday mornings, Mary and Joe like to sleep until 9:00 A.M., which is a real treat since they are up much earlier on other days. Their neighbor insists on cutting his grass or working on his house early Saturday morning (7:30–8:00), disturbing their one morning in the week when they can sleep late.**

5. *Behavioral Rehearsal:*

    A. *Selection:* The teacher will select three groups of students to role play.

    B. *Role Play:* Each group will perform one of the following three situations. The students can suggest other suitable role plays, if time permits.

        – Over the past few weeks, Carl has borrowed money from his friends Fred and Paul. He owes them a large sum. They have told him several times that they want to be paid back. Although Carl has promised many times to pay the money back, he has not returned any of it. Now, Fred and Paul are really mad and want to retaliate in some way.

        – Carrie's shoelace was untied, which caused her to trip and fall in the hall at school. Janine, who was standing with a group of girls, saw what happened to Carrie, pointed at her and started laughing. Carrie got up and shouted, "I'll get you, Janine!"

        – Cody was just opening his front door when a carload of boys drove by and started firing a gun. His friend's eight-year-old sister was hit by a bullet. Cody told his friend who the shooter was and now his friend is set on getting revenge.

    C. *Completion:* The teacher will acknowledge that the role play is complete if the role plays are done correctly. If corrections are needed, the teacher will have the students redo them with the necessary changes.

    D. *Reinforcers:* The teacher will thank students for their participation and their excellent performance. The other, non-acting students will applaud.

    E. *Discussion:* After each role play, the teacher can encourage class discussion of the deeds and feelings which were causing the need for revenge or retaliation by asking the following questions:

        ❯ **What negative or harmful consequences could the acts of revenge have upon all persons involved?**

        ❯ **How can a person deal with the deeds and feelings which initiate the need for revenge in a way that does not provoke further problems and increased violence?**

6. *Practice:* The teacher will distribute copies of the worksheet "Find the Right Word" and ask students to complete the worksheet in class and to share their examples of "when and how this skill could help you."

7. ***Independent Use:*** The teacher will hand out copies of the worksheet "Revenge—Then and Now" for students to complete at home and bring back to class for discussion.

8. ***Continuation:*** The teacher will remind students that whenever they are upset by what another person says or does, and feel that revenge is the way to respond, this skill will help them look for and find other solutions to relieve their feelings without creating additional problems, more serious incidents or even violence. This is a useful skill for young people and adults to have and apply throughout their entire life.

Name _____ Date _____

FIND THE RIGHT WORD

Directions: Use the words listed below to complete the following sentences:

consequences	**strategy**	**revenge**
deed	**act**	**provoke**
responsible	**non-violent**	**feeling**

1. Think about why you want to have _____.

2. Decide which _____ or act disturbed you.

3. Identify what you are _____.

4. Consider what may have caused the other person to _____ as they did.

5. Consider the _____ of any acts of revenge.

6. Think of _____ solutions.

7. If necessary, talk with a _____ person about your feelings.

8. Plan a _____ that will not _____ further problems or violence.

In this space, write one example (at least two paragraphs long) showing when and how the skill of choosing the right word could help you.

Name _____ Date _____

REVENGE—THEN AND NOW

Directions: Describe a situation with siblings or friends when you felt the need for revenge. Explain what you did *then* and how you might react differently now using a strategy that does not cause further problems and uses the skill components.

REVENGE SITUATION:

How I reacted *THEN:*

How I would react *NOW:*

Supporting Family Harmony

Behavioral Objective: Students will learn how to support family harmony by developing understanding of each other's needs and by refining their communication and listening skills.

Directed Lesson:

1. **Establish the Need:** During the last two decades, the number of dysfunctional families has increased substantially. But even in two parent families strife within and among families has grown and the number of divorces has increased markedly. Adolescents have frequently been at the center of strife within the family. Young people need to develop an appropriate understanding of each other's needs and to refine their listening and communication skills and use them to build good family relationships and to support family harmony.

2. **Introduction:** The teacher will read the following story to the class:

   Kimberly is a fourteen-year-old who has a brother, Alan, 18, and younger sister Karen, 9. Kimberly's mother and father have been married for nearly a quarter of a century and are working hard to send Alan, who recently graduated from high school, to the college of his choice, Texas A & M. Since he is an out-of-state student, the tuition costs are double what they would be for him to attend an in-state school. Early one evening, Kimberly overhears her mother and father "debating" whether Alan could or should go to Texas rather than an in-state school because she indicates to the father that "she had made a promise to Kimberly that she could go to a private girls school as a high school student." The father responds that he never knew anything of it. The argument becomes heated and is not resolved, due to the father having to leave for work. Later, at breakfast, prior to Kim's leaving for school, it is apparent that Kim's mother is upset. She is "short" and irritable. When she asks Kim about her term paper, Kim becomes defensive and says that "she will get it done in due time," and becomes angry, slams the door and leaves the house for school.

   Later that evening, at the dinner table, there appears to be some uneasiness present. While having dessert, Kim abruptly says to Alan, "You know, if you go to Texas A & M, I won't be able to do what I wanted to do. I don't understand why you just can't be satisfied to go to a college close to home!" Alan is startled by the comment and replies "What's it to you?" and leaves the table. Then Kim says to her mother, "You promised me that I would go to Taylor's Academy, Mom."

   The teacher then asks the following questions:

   ▶ **Did Kim handle this situation properly? If yes, why? If no, why not?**

71

) **Was the timing of her comments appropriate? Why? Why not?**

) **Was her choice of words the best ones?**

) **Did she consider other persons in her family before making comments?**

The teacher then reinforces the discussion by placing suggestions on the board relative to:

Individual Actions (Verbal, Non-verbal)
Choice of Words (Voice, Tone, Volume)
Timing
Feelings
Respect

All these items will help to maintain and improve family harmony.

3. ***Identify the Skill Components:*** Write the following skill components on the board or on sentence strips:

1. Identify the problem.
2. Decide on the outcome desired.
3. Consider feelings, viewpoints, and positions of others.
4. Consider the best time to raise an issue.
5. Consider the words you will use.
6. Keep smiling.
7. Determine when you will discuss the subject.
8. Consider possible reaction(s) of others
9. Listen carefully.
10. Decide on a strategy.
11. Follow through.

4. ***Model the Skill:*** The teacher will select one boy and one girl to demonstrate how the choice of words can lead to a confrontation. He/she will use the scenario in the introduction as a basis to portray a "family matter." The teacher will select the best approach to resolving a "family matter" by using the skill components.

5. ***Behavioral Rehearsal:***

A. *Selection:* The teacher will identify four groups of five students each to role play a different "family matter."

B. *Role Play:* Each group will role play either the scenario described in the story of the introduction or a similar scenario of their own choice, providing the teacher agrees. The role play will involve the correct choice of words, the best use of non-verbal gestures, and how to select the time and location for airing an objection to a family decision without starting a controversy.

C. *Completion:* After each role play, the teacher will reinforce correct behavior, identify inappropriate behaviors, and have the students reenact the role play with corrections. If no corrections, the role play is complete.

D. *Reinforcers:* The teacher and class will applaud each group of actors and will point out and praise special accomplishments.

E. *Discussion:* The teacher will start the discussion by asking the following questions:

> **What would you suggest to do to develop necessary understanding for preserving and supporting harmony in the family?**

> **How important is it to choose the right time and use well-prepared words to discuss a controversial issue and still keep harmony?**

> **How important is it to use face and hand signs carefully and to your advantage?**

6. ***Practice:*** The teacher will distribute the worksheet entitled "Controversy" for completion and discussion in class.

7. ***Independent Use:*** The teacher will ask the students to complete the worksheet "My Family and I" at home and return it in two weeks for discussion in class.

8. ***Continuation:*** The teacher will review some positive approaches which can be used to create and preserve family harmony several times during the year since it is a most important skill for the students to practice to improve and maintain good family relationships. The teacher will communicate this idea and the importance of this skill to the class and also indicate that this skill will be useful in later life when they have a family of their own.

Name _____ Date _____

CONTROVERSY

Directions: Think of a family situation that occurred at home and led to a long and noisy discussion and finally to controversy. (If you cannot recall any such situation, make one up.)

Describe the situation using the following headings:

1. Persons present: _____

2. Incident: _____

3. Argument: _____

Tell how you would promote (1) harmony and (2) controversy using the following items. Use the skill components to explain your actions.

Items	Harmony	Controversy
1. Location:		
2. Words:		
3. Actions:		
4. Body signs:		
5. Understanding:		
6. Feelings:		
7. Timing:		
8. Respect:		

State below which of the skill components were used and how they did help.

Name _____ Date _____

MY FAMILY AND I

Directions: During the next two weeks, describe your own actions whenever a family discussion starts to heat up or when a dispute occurs between family members. Pay special attention to your own actions and tell whether they preserved family harmony or promoted controversy. Use the skill components to grade your actions from one (1) to ten (10), with ten indicating that they created full harmony. Describe a minimum of three situations in the following manner. (If no situations occur during those two weeks, relate earlier situations.)

Situation:

    a. Persons: _____

    b. Location: _____

    c. Timing: _____

    d. Dispute: _____

My actions and thoughts: _____

My feelings: _____

Feelings expressed by others: _____

Grade I give myself: _____

The skill components I used: _____

_____

I will improve my grade by: _____

_____

Situation:

    a. Persons: _____

    b. Location: _____

    c. Timing: _____

    d. Dispute: _____

My actions and thoughts: _____

My feelings: _____

Feelings expressed by others: _____

Grade I give myself: _____

The skill components I used: _____

_____

I will improve my grade by: _____

_____

NOTE: For added situations, use the same format on the back of this page and, if needed, an extra page.

Understanding to Distinguish Discipline from Punishment

Behavioral Objective: Students will learn to understand and distinguish discipline from punishment and to realize that discipline is exercised by following strict rules, which might differ depending on circumstance and environment.

Directed Lesson:

1. **Establish the Need:** Young people as well as adults often fail to distinguish between punishment and discipline. Punishment is a way of exerting power over another. Parents, for instance, use punishment to control their children's behavior. Punishment then becomes a penalty exerted by the "power" person to the wrongdoer. Discipline, on the other hand, teaches children responsibility for their behavior through the application of appropriate consequences for certain misbehaviors. Discipline creates motivation for self-control. Rules which relate to health, safety and governmental laws are necessary to provide an environment in which people can coexist. Home rules, school rules, and work rules, which may be negotiated at times, are necessary to keep discipline depending upon respective environments and circumstances and also to ensure coexistence.

2. **Introduction:** The teacher will ask the students to label the following examples as discipline, punishment, or rules and to be ready to explain why. (These examples can be written on the board or copied on paper to hand out to each student.)

   Example 1   **Mary, 14 years old, threw things (books, clothes, etc.) around her room because she was upset about something. When her mother saw the mess, she said that since Mary made the mess, Mary would have to put the room back in order herself.**

   Example 2   **Gideon, who has had a driver's license for one year, was driving 40 miles an hour in a 25 miles an hour business area. He was given a ticket, fined $100.00 and received two points on his driver's license.**

   Example 3   **John came in from school and threw his jacket and bookbag on the sofa. When his father came home and saw where the jacket and bookbag were, he began to yell at John, saying that he's old enough (13) to know what to do with his belongings. His dad then took off his belt to use on John.**

   Answers: Ex. 1 = discipline; Ex. 2 = rules; Ex. 3 = punishment

3. **Identify the Skill Components:** Write the following skill components on the board or on sentence strips.

1. Analyze the behavior of all involved.
2. Consider the consequences.
3. Decide if discipline was missing.
4. Decide if punishment is appropriate.
5. If yes, accept it without objection.
6. Learn discipline through self-control.
7. Realize the importance of discipline.
8. Use self-control.

4. **Model the Skill:** The teacher will relate an experience from his/her past which will allow him/her to use the skill components to model the skill.

5. **Behavioral Rehearsal:**

   A. *Selection:* The teacher will select pairs of students to role play.

   B. *Role Play:* Students will be asked to suggest examples of inappropriate behaviors or broken rules. One student will role play the parent or other "in charge" person, and the other student will role play the person who is disciplined or punished and who will use the skill components.

   C. *Completion:* After each role play, the teacher will reinforce correct behavior, identify inappropriate behaviors, and if necessary ask the students to reenact the role play with corrections. If no corrections are needed, the role play is complete.

   D. *Reinforcers:* The teacher and class will acknowledge the efforts of the role playing students with applause and compliments.

   E. *Discussion:* The teacher will use questions such as the following to encourage discussion about the need for discipline:

   ▶ **Why is discipline necessary?**
   ▶ **When should discipline begin?**
   ▶ **What is the difference between discipline and punishment?**
   ▶ **What are self-discipline and self-control?**
   ▶ **How can self-discipline and self-control be beneficial to you?**

6. **Practice:** The teacher will distribute copies of the worksheet "Discipline, Punishment, Rules" to complete in class and have them share the answers and discuss them in class.

7. **Independent Use:** The teacher will distribute copies of the worksheet "Rules" for students to complete at home and ask them to return their completed worksheets in one week to share and discuss in class.

8. **Continuation:** The teacher will emphasize the importance of discipline, which is needed in order to live together in harmony in the family, school, community, and while at work or play. Discipline is an integral part of living and therefore rules have to be made and followed. To do so, self-control is most important.

Name _____ Date _____

DISCIPLINE, PUNISHMENT, RULES

Directions: After each statement below, determine if it is discipline, punishment, or if a rule has been ignored (broken). Write your decision on the blank.

1. You cannot play video games because you did not get an "A" on your spelling test.

   _____

2. The Health Department inspector fined a restaurant owner $200.00 because the food handlers were not wearing hairnets.

   _____

3. Because you earned a "D" on a math test, your mother said you must work with a tutor every weekday for one hour after school until you can get at least a "B."

   _____

4. Mary was 1/2 hour late past her curfew. Her mother slapped her across the face several times.

   _____

5. Sammy didn't cut the grass on Saturday as he was told to do by his dad; therefore, he had to do it on Sunday afternoon causing him to miss a baseball game.

   _____

6. Bob, 16 years old, received a ticket for going through a "four-way stop" intersection without stopping. He had to appear, with his parent, in juvenile court and was fined $50.00.

   _____

   At home, his father said that:

   (a) Bob would have to earn the $50.00 to repay him for paying the fine in court.

   _____

   (b) Bob is "grounded" for a month.

   _____

Name _____ Date _____

NO TURN ON RED

RULES

YIELD

Directions: Write definitions of each of the following words on a separate sheet of paper

discipline	punishment	rules
control	power	penalty
teach	responsibility	behavior
appropriate	self-discipline	self-control
necessary	consequences	limit

Directions: Sometimes it is difficult to accept and understand the need for rules at home, at school, at work, and at other places. Think of one rule for each selected environment below. Write down the rule, tell why you don't like the rule, then think of as many reasons as possible why the rule is necessary.

1. HOME RULE: _____

_____

I don't like it because _____

_____

_____

_____

It is necessary because _____

_____

_____

_____

2. SCHOOL RULE: _____

_____

I don't like it because _____

_____

_____

Rules *(cont'd)*

It is necessary because _____

_____

_____

_____

3. WORK RULE: _____

_____

I don't like it because _____

_____

_____

_____

It is necessary because _____

_____

_____

_____

4. TRAFFIC RULE: _____

I don't like it because _____

_____

_____

_____

It is necessary because _____

_____

_____

_____

Understanding the Needs of the Elderly

Behavioral Objective: Students will learn about and understand the needs of the elderly, what constitutes elderly mistreatment, and how to help elderly family members.

Directed Lesson:

1. **Establish the Need:** Sometimes, teenagers find their home routines disrupted due to an elderly family member who can no longer live independently and must move into a relative's home. Not only are routines disrupted, but distribution of space and activities may be curtailed and other habits changed to accommodate the elderly relative. The elderly relative may have diminished mental or physical capabilities which require assistance for the elementary tasks such as eating, dressing, and so on. The loss of space, change in routines and habits, etc. may cause a certain degree of resentment by the teen toward the elderly person, resulting in unkind words, rough treatment, neglect, and even injury or death. Young people need to understand that the needs of the elderly may be very different from their own; that by showing respect, being kind, and helping to provide for their care, they will not only make the elderly person feel welcome and secure, but also help themselves build self-esteem, demonstrate their level of responsibility, and have a valuable learning experience since many elderly persons have interesting and useful information to share.

2. **Introduction:** The teacher shares the following story of Grandma Lily:

   Grandma Lily came to live with her daughter, Mary, son-in-law, and two grandchildren. Her grandson, John, is 11 and her granddaughter, Kaye, is 17. The family did not have an extra bedroom, so the TV room was turned into a bedroom for Grandma Lily. Both grandchildren are upset that the TV room was lost to Grandma Lily. They resent her moving in and do not hide their feelings about the situation.

   Grandma Lily needs assistance with bathing and getting dressed, and someone has to prepare her meals for her. She often talks to herself and sometimes acts confused and forgets where she is, especially if she does not eat well or misses a meal. And, she doesn't like being left alone for long periods of time.

   Since Mary and her husband both work outside the home, John and Kaye are expected to look after Grandma Lily after school and on Saturdays and Sundays when both parents are gone.

   Because John and Kaye resent her being there, they sometimes forget to check on Grandma Lily, neglect to give her a meal, as required, and pretend not to hear her when she calls. Therefore, Grandma Lily misses meals and becomes weaker and more dependent for assistance.

One day, when John and Kaye were supposed to be taking care of Grandma Lily, she wandered out of the house. The police found her in a deteriorated condition several blocks from home. The police took her to a hospital for care. When Mary and her husband came home, they asked John and Kaye how things had been with Grandma Lily. They replied that everything was okay and that Grandma Lily had not bothered them. Mary went to the door of Grandma Lily's room. . . .

The teacher will ask the students to tell what happens when Mary looks into Grandma Lily's room. The teacher will also ask if they have ever had to help care for an elderly person. Other questions that will help to stimulate class discussion include:

▶ **What suggestions do you have for Mary and her family and Grandma Lily?**

▶ **Should elderly people expect their grown children to take care of them when they can no longer live on their own?**

▶ **How do the needs of an elderly person differ from those of young people? Why?**

3. ***Identify the Skill Components:*** Write the following skill components on the board or on sentence strips:

1. Think about the needs of the elderly.
2. Respect their limitations.
3. Show empathy.
4. Try to understand their feelings.
5. Learn from their experience.
6. Understand the consequences of neglect.
7. Share in taking care of their needs.
8. Be patient.

4. ***Model the Skill:*** The teacher will model having an elderly mother who is bedridden living with him/her. He/she will model how he/she reacts to the mother's requests for things to be brought to her. The think-aloud method can be used to demonstrate the use of the skill components, or the teacher will ask a student to take the mother's part to help with the modeling.

5. ***Behavioral Rehearsal:***

A. *Selection:* The teacher will select as many students as needed to role play the story of Grandma Lily.

B. *Role Play:* The students will role play the story of Grandma Lily to show how the skill components could have helped everyone adjust better to the situation.

C. *Completion:* Following the role play, the teacher will reinforce correct behaviors, identify inappropriate behaviors, and re-enact role play with corrections, if needed. If there are no corrections, the role play is complete.

D. *Reinforcers:* The role players will be rewarded with applause from the teacher and the class.

E. *Discussion:* The teacher will lead the discussion with questions such as:

> ◗ **In a situation like this, how can better communication help?**
>
> ◗ **What extra burdens are put on a family?**
>
> ◗ **Are elderly people the only ones who may need this kind of family support?**
>
> ◗ **What about handicapped people or those severely injured?**
>
> ◗ **Would the skill components be helpful in other situations?**

6. ***Practice:*** The teacher will distribute copies of the worksheet "Guess Who's Coming to Live with Us!" for students to complete in class and share.

7. ***Independent Use:*** The teacher will hand out the worksheet "Time Together" for students to complete at home and return to class for sharing and discussion. They may want to discuss this assignment with a parent to get some ideas.

8. ***Continuation:*** The teacher will remind students that elderly persons are not the only ones who may need special care, assistance, and consideration. Persons of all ages with temporary or permanent injuries or handicaps may require similar attention. When providing such care, the students will realize that they gain much satisfaction, increased self-esteem, insight and enjoyment by sharing their time in this way.

Name _____ Date _____

"GUESS WHO'S COMING TO LIVE WITH US!"

Directions: Write a description of an elderly person (real or made-up) who is coming to live with your family. Be sure to describe things such as age, mental and physical abilities or limitations, space requirements, assistance needs, and so on

_____ is coming to our house. He/she

(descriptive name, such as Grandma Lily)

Use the following suggestions to make a "care plan," such as started under example for Sunday.

- ▶ Understand the feelings of the elderly person and why he/she feels this way.
- ▶ Recognize the physical and/or mental limitations, if any.
- ▶ Contact day care programs for the elderly about programs and assistance.
- ▶ Make a schedule of who does what and when.
- ▶ Share the care among all responsible family members.
- ▶ Ask those outside the immediate family to help.
- ▶ Find a reliable person to assist.

CARE PLAN

Example:

S	M	T	W	T	F	S
9:00 Mother						
10:00 Church						
11:30 Aunt Esther's house						
5:30 so on						

Name _____ Date _____

TIME TOGETHER

Directions: List 4 activities which a young person and an elderly person could engage in together in a positive, enjoyable manner. Tell how each activity will benefit both the young person and the elderly person.

#1. _____

Benefits:

#2.. _____

Benefits:

#3. _____

Benefits:

#4. _____

Benefits:

Coping with Stressful Family Situations

Behavioral Objective: Students will learn to identify the behavior of individual family members when under stress, which could result in a dangerous or violent situation, and how to cope with such situations.

Directed Lesson:

1. **Establish the Need:** In today's world, conditions arise or are present in some families which cause dangerous and sometimes violent situations, such as job loss, chemical abuse, drinking, divorce, and so on. Students need to learn to recognize and cope with stressful family situations and violent behavior.

2. **Introduction:** The teacher will read the following story entitled "An Elephant in the Living Room."

   Imagine an ordinary living room . . . chairs, couch, coffee table, a TV set, and, in the middle, a

   LARGE GRAY ELEPHANT

   The ELEPHANT stands there, shifting from one foot to another and slowly swaying from side to side.

   Imagine also the people that live in the house; you, along with your mother and father and maybe some sisters and brothers. People have to go through the living room many times a day and you watch as they walk through it very . . . carefully . . . around . . . the ELEPHANT. No one ever says anything about the ELEPHANT. They avoid the swinging trunk and just walk around it. Since no one ever talks about the ELEPHANT, you know that you're not supposed to talk about it either. And you don't.

   But sometimes you wonder why nobody is saying anything or why nobody is doing anything to move the ELEPHANT. After all, it's a very big elephant and it's very hard to keep walking around it all the time, and people are getting very tired of doing so. You wonder if maybe there is something wrong with you. But you just keep wondering, keep walking around it, keep worrying and wishing that there was somebody to talk to about the ELEPHANT.

   The teacher will remark at the end of the story that living in a family where drinking is a problem is a lot like living with an ELEPHANT in the living room. The teacher will then use the following questions to discuss the story:

   ▶ **Who can explain the meaning of the story?**

86

> ❱ Is a "drinking problem" the only "Elephant" that could be in the family's living room? Name some others.

> ❱ Which one of these problems (problems named by the students) could lead to violence?

> ❱ How might such problems affect the child(ren) in a family? (Some possible responses could be that the children would be lonely, depressed, isolated, angry, ashamed, etc.)

The teacher will tell the students that although they may feel helpless in such situations, there are some steps that they can take which will help them to cope with the situation.

3. ***Identify the Skill Components:*** Write the following skill components on the board or on sentence strips.

   1. Analyze the family problem.
   2. Determine how much suffering there is.
   3. Determine if this is a short or long time problem.
   4. Analyze the effects on you.
   5. Think about your options for coping.
   6. Decide if it is best to ignore or face the problem.
   7. Decide if you need help.
   8. If yes, ask a trusted adult.
   9. If no, plan how you can cope with the situation.
   10. Follow through with your decision.

4. ***Model the Skill:*** The teacher will model the skill and use the skill components in a divorce situation. The teacher will portray how a teen will react when he/she learns of the parents' decision to divorce. He/she will use the skill components to demonstrate the ability to cope with the situation. The teacher will use the "think aloud" method or ask a student to portray a friend with whom the teen is sharing the problem.

5. ***Behavioral Rehearsal:***

   A. *Selection:* The teacher will select the number of students required for each of the role plays.

   B. *Role Play:* As time permits, the students can role play the following situations:
   - Darlene's older brother is always hitting her. Lately, the hits have been harder, leaving bruises.
   - Steve's father comes home very drunk and becomes angry when he notices that Steve did not take out the garbage as he had told him to do earlier in the day.
   - Mary's mom and dad were having another fight. Mary really hates it when they yell and scream at each other.
   - Sam was looking in his brother's dresser for some clean socks to wear. While looking for the socks, Sam finds what looks like "crack" cocaine and a handgun.

– George lives with his mother. She is the sole support for George and his sister. His mother comes home from work one day and begins slamming doors, kicking at the furniture, and breaking things. When he asks what's wrong, she screams at him that she has lost her job.

C. *Completion:* As each role play is finished, the teacher and class will decide if the role play is correct and if the skill components were used. If not, the role play should be re-enacted with corrections; if there are no corrections needed, the role play is complete.

D. *Reinforcers:* Applause after each role play and praise from the teacher will acknowledge a job well done by the participants.

E. *Discussion:* The teacher-led discussion after each role play should include questions such as:

   ▶ **How prevalent are such occurrences in families?**

   ▶ **How serious can such a problem become?**

   ▶ **Do you know anyone who has experienced such a problem? What did they do about the situation?**

   ▶ **If they had learned to apply the skill components, would the outcome of their situations have been different?**

   ▶ **Would it help to use the skill components in such a situation?**

6. *Practice:* The teacher will distribute the worksheet "Coping Word Search" and ask the students to complete the word search and share answers with others who may have trouble finding all the words.

7. *Independent Use:* Students will interview a parent or other family adult about a difficult family situation which they or someone they know had as a teenager. During the interview, students will ask the questions: What was the problem? How did it affect them or you? and What did they or you do about it? The teacher will ask the students to share their interviews with the class in one week. At that time, the teacher could ask the students, **Based on the knowledge of the skill components, if this happened to you now, how would you deal with the same problem?**

8. *Continuation:* The teacher will emphasize that difficult situations and problem behaviors can occur in any family, regardless of location, economic status, race, religion, and so on. The teacher should stress that blaming one's self for the irrational and violent behaviors of another family member is not healthy. Students should be reminded that the skill components can help them to explore their options and can guide them to the safest and best solution.

Name _____   Date _____

COPING WORD SEARCH

Directions: Find the following words. They may be found forward, backward, diagonally, horizontally, or vertically.

manage	decide	family	effect
situation	analyze	stressful	options
problem	think	violent	help
decision	determine	dangerous	cope

A	B	M	V	V	O	P	T	I	O	N	S	B	V
N	L	S	I	T	U	A	T	I	O	N	F	J	I
A	T	I	U	E	D	G	S	O	H	K	I	G	O
L	J	S	T	R	E	S	S	F	U	L	R	H	L
Y	L	K	H	D	C	T	U	C	B	C	O	P	E
Z	Y	U	I	C	I	A	O	K	P	T	H	R	N
E	W	L	N	Y	D	D	R	L	X	C	Z	O	T
Z	M	N	K	M	E	J	E	O	R	G	S	B	B
N	V	D	G	F	L	H	G	F	N	A	Q	L	Y
D	E	T	E	R	M	I	N	E	W	E	P	E	L
X	P	C	H	E	X	M	A	N	A	G	E	M	I
P	W	O	V	Q	C	I	D	R	G	M	Q	D	M
O	A	P	B	Y	F	C	E	F	F	E	C	T	A
Z	D	E	C	I	S	I	O	N	F	S	U	E	F

COPING WORD SEARCH

Answer Key

Directions: Find the following words. They may be found forward, backward, diagonally, horizontally, or vertically.

manage	decide	family	effect
situation	analyze	stressful	options
problem	think	violent	help
decision	determine	dangerous	cope

A	B	M	V	V	O	P	T	I	O	N	S	B	V
N	L	S	I	T	U	A	T	I	O	N	F	J	I
A	T	I	U	E	D	G	S	O	H	K	I	G	O
L	J	S	T	R	E	S	S	F	U	L	R	H	L
Y	L	K	H	D	C	T	U	C	B	C	O	P	E
Z	Y	U	I	C	I	A	O	K	P	T	H	R	N
E	W	L	N	Y	D	D	R	L	X	C	Z	O	T
Z	M	N	K	M	E	J	E	O	R	G	S	B	B
N	V	D	G	F	L	H	G	F	N	A	Q	L	Y
D	E	T	E	R	M	I	N	E	W	E	P	E	L
X	P	C	H	E	X	M	A	N	A	G	E	M	I
P	W	O	V	Q	C	I	D	R	G	M	Q	D	M
O	A	P	B	Y	F	C	E	F	F	E	C	T	A
Z	D	E	C	I	S	I	O	N	F	S	U	E	F

Understanding Sibling Rivalry

Behavioral Objective: Students will understand sibling rivalry and will learn to reduce their zeal to compete with each other for attention and favors from parents and others and to share their possessions peacefully.

Directed Lesson:

1. ***Establish the Need:*** Although some sibling rivalry is a normal part of growing up, excessive competitiveness, which can lead to fighting and a permanent rift in relationships, is not. Siblings need to understand that equality in attention, favors, possessions, and so on is not always possible and that extreme or violent reactions are not beneficial to anyone. However, human behavior is not always logical and altercations between siblings do occur. Students need to understand the reasons for sibling rivalry, recognize the signs of and specific reasons for sibling rivalry, and be aware of ways to end it in a peaceful manner.

2. ***Introduction:*** The teacher will read this story to the class:

   The Smith family consists of two working parents, a one-year-old girl named Tina, a 13-year-old boy named Roger, and an 18-year-old named Nick. After being the youngest child for 12 years, Roger resents the attention Tina requires and gets from his parents and others and he thinks that his older brother has too many privileges like having a later curfew, not having to baby-sit as often and having nicer clothes.

   Nick does have nice clothes because he works and uses some of his earnings to buy nice things. Nick is away from home a lot because of his job and because of his involvement in high school sports such as wrestling and football; therefore he does not baby-sit with Tina very much. And, due to his age, good grades, etc., his parents have given him an age-appropriate curfew.

   Roger and Nick seem to argue and fight often because Roger "borrows" Nick's things without asking and is always complaining about what he sees as special treatment towards Nick by his parents.

   On this particular day, Roger was supposed to come straight home from school because the regular babysitter had to leave early. Roger's mom had told him to take over the care of Tina until she gets home from work.

   Roger had to stay after school for being late to school that morning. Roger had spent too much time going through his clothes and then Nick's clothes to find something to wear—one of Nick's sweaters that was really sharp, but also too big for Roger. Roger didn't care—baggy was in.

When Roger got home, the babysitter was gone and Nick was with Tina. When Nick heard Roger coming in, he started yelling at Roger about the fact that Roger's lateness had made him miss football practice and that the coach was going to be mad. Before Roger could slip upstairs to take off Nick's sweater, Nick looked up and saw that Roger was wearing his sweater—without permission!

The teacher will ask the students to predict what will happen next.

After the predictions, the teacher will ask the following questions:

> ▶ **What could be considered "normal" sibling rivalry between Roger and his siblings Tina and Nick?**

> ▶ **What part is excessive?**

> ▶ **What could be done to help Roger (and his siblings) to understand what is happening, especially to Roger?**

> ▶ **Why is it happening and how can it be dealt with in a more peaceable way?**

3. *Identify the Skill Components:* Write the following skill components on the board:

1. Determine the seriousness of sibling rivalry.
2. Consider the reasons for this rivalry.
3. Express your feelings calmly.
4. Analyze everybody's feelings.
5. Listen carefully to those involved.
6. Remain open to suggestions.
7. Decide on a solution beneficial to all.
8. Reduce sibling rivalry through understanding.
9. Involve a responsible "third party," if necessary.

4. *Model the Skill:* The teacher will share a personal story concerning a case of sibling rivalry from his/her youth. The teacher will demonstrate how the skill components could have helped him/her to cope with his/her case of sibling rivalry.

5. *Behavioral Rehearsal:*

A. *Selection:* The teacher will select two or three students to role play the situation in the introduction.

B. *Role Play:* Students will show how the sibling rivalry in the Smith family could be dealt with through the use of the skill components. Other situations could be suggested by students and teacher and role played as time permits.

C. *Completion:* After the role play is finished, the teacher and students will determine if the role play was done correctly and if skill components were used to bring about the appropriate behaviors. If not, the role play will be redone using the skill components. If there are no corrections, the role play is complete.

    D. *Reinforcers:* The teacher and peers will applaud and give other forms of praise. They will acknowledge the efforts and cooperation of the role playing students.

    E. *Discussion:* The teacher will encourage discussion about sibling rivalry through such questions as:

- **What are some signs of sibling rivalry?**
- **How much rivalry is considered "normal" and how much is "extreme"?**
- **How can sibling rivalry damage a family?**
- **Who should take responsibility to resolve sibling rivalry?**

6. **Practice:** The teacher will have students complete the worksheet "Problems with Siblings" and share their responses in class.

7. **Independent Use:** The teacher will ask the students to complete the "Our Shields" project at home and return it to class in one week for sharing. At school, students can devise a clever way to display the family groupings of sibling shields.

8. **Continuation:** The teacher will point out that fortunately, in most cases, after siblings grow up they will become close friends; therefore, the earlier positive bonding begins, the fewer conflicts will arise and the family can experience more happy times.

Name _____   Date _____

PROBLEMS WITH SIBLINGS

Directions: Describe how each of the following situations that could cause "problems with siblings" could be resolved peacefully. Remember to apply the skill components.

1. Being compared to another sibling.

2. Feeling left out by family members.

3. Wanting to use the same item at the same time.

4. Belongings taken without permission.

5. Made responsible for the actions of a sibling.

6. Parents always give you the responsibility of taking care of younger siblings.

7. Feeling you are being "picked on."

Name _____ Date _____

OUR SHIELDS

Directions: Design one shield for yourself and one for each brother and/or sister. (If you are an only child, choose someone close to your age who is a member of your extended family.) In each quadrant of the individual's shield, write a positive characteristic of that person. Use the pattern below.

(Name and age of sibling or close friend on top of shield)

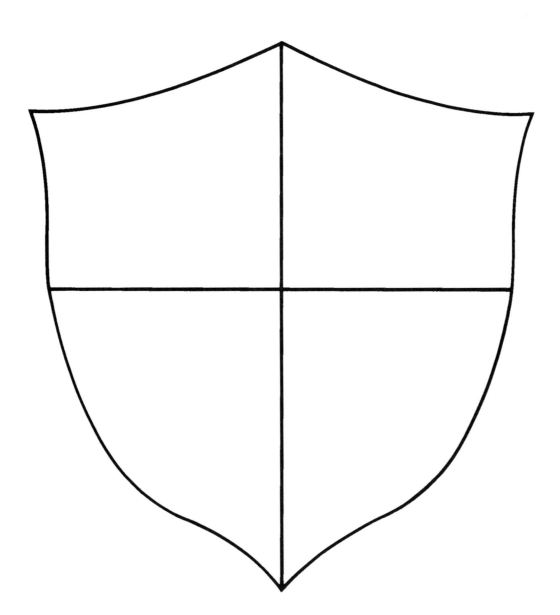

Understanding Violence in the Family

Behavioral Objective: Students will learn about various types of violence in the family, what can be done to avoid it, and how to protect family members from violence created by another family member.

Directed Lesson:

1. **Establish the Need:** Unfortunately, violence in families is a frequent occurrence in many cultures of today. Young people who are exposed to family violence suffer from anxiety, exhibit the effects of stress caused by trauma, and can be affected for life. It is believed that youngsters who grow up in violent homes are more likely to repeat this violence in their own families and other relationships. Youth must realize that violence in families is not the norm, does not belong in families, and should not be tolerated and that there are ways to deal with it. It is important for young people to be aware of the frequency of violence, the perpetrators, the circumstances of the violence and to know when and how to seek help, either from within the family or from an outside source. Sometimes, having a trusted adult in whom they can confide can get them through the difficult times.

2. **Introduction:** The teacher will use the following story to introduce the topic.

   Sandra's mother was sitting in the living room talking on the telephone to her friend, Mrs. Baker, who lives several houses down the street. Mrs. Baker has expressed concern for Sandra's mother (and Sandra, too) because she frequently sees bruises and black eyes on Sandra's mother. Mrs. Baker has said she would help in any way she could.

   While her mother was on the phone, her father unexpectedly came home. Mother said good-bye to Mrs. Baker and hung up the phone. Sandra's father became instantly angry because dinner was not ready. When her mother tried to explain that it would soon be ready and that he was home earlier than usual, her father only became more angry and slapped her mother once across the face. He then grabbed Sandra by the arm and pushed her into the bathroom and locked her in as he usually did when he was getting ready to really assault her mother. Sandra could hear her mother begging him not to beat her again as the father dragged the mother toward the basement.

   The teacher will ask the following questions:

   ▶ **How does this kind of violence (domestic violence or spousal abuse) affect members of the family?**

   ▶ **Who is being harmed by this violence? How?**

> ❿ **Mrs. Baker offered to help. What could she do?**
>
> ❿ **Is there anything Sandra and/or her mother could do about this violent family condition?**

3. ***Identify the Skill Components:*** Write the following skill components on the board or on sentence strips:

1. Analyze the reason for the outbreak of violence.
2. Compare the situation to previous ones.
3. Think about the frequency and severity.
4. Analyze how this affects you and others.
5. Define your feelings.
6. Decide if help is needed.
7. Determine whom to ask for help.
8. Discuss the situation.
9. Consider your options.
10. Choose a plan of action.
11. Follow through.

4. ***Model the Skill:*** The teacher will tell the students about a youngster who suffers from the actions of a violent sibling. The teacher will use the skill components to demonstrate how this youngster can avoid the continued violent behavior of the sibling and protect him/herself when such behavior reoccurs.

5. ***Behavioral Rehearsal:***

   A. *Selection:* The teacher will select two and three students as needed for the role plays.

   B. *Role Play:* The teacher will ask three students to role play the scene from the introduction and two students the example from the "Model the Skill" section. Other role plays can be suggested by the students themselves or by the teacher, if time permits.

   C. *Completion:* After each role play, the teacher will reinforce correct behaviors, identify inappropriate behaviors and have the students re-enact the role play with corrections, if needed. If there are no corrections, the role play is complete.

   D. *Reinforcers:* The teacher and peers will thank the students for their input and participation in the role plays and will praise their performances.

   E. *Discussion:* Through questions and discussion, the teacher should have the class identify the reasons that would provoke violence in the family. The class will discuss how violence in the family affects all family members, what the signs of family violence are, what happens when everyone "looks the other way," where a person can get help, what agencies offer assistance, and so on.

6. ***Practice:*** The teacher will divide the class into groups of three to five students and give each group the worksheet "Family Violence" to complete by discussing and writing a plan of action or solution. All groups will share their suggestions for an action plan after completion of the assignment.

7. ***Independent Use:*** The teacher will ask the students to do research on the topic of family violence and to write a 3–5 page paper with references. Students should cite at least two agencies that assist persons experiencing family violence. This paper should be completed and brought to class in one week for discussion.

8. ***Continuation:*** The teacher will emphasize that, in many cases, outside intervention is needed in family violence situations. However, students can learn how necessary and important it is to stop the cycle of repeating family violence from one generation to the next and that violence in the family is not a normal behavioral occurrence.

Name _____ Date _____

FAMILY VIOLENCE

Directions: After reading the story below, discuss what is happening, and what the family member(s) can do to reduce or eliminate the violence. Use the rest of this page and the back to complete the assignment by writing a plan of action to resolve the problem of this family violence.

Mrs. Jones is a divorced mother of three children, ages 6, 8, and 14. She is the sole support of the family and must work long and hard to provide for herself and the children. She often gets angry and, at times, is both verbally and physically abusive to her children. On this particular Saturday, Mrs. Jones comes home from work very tired and finds that the children have not "straightened up" the house as she had specifically instructed them to do before she left for work. In fact, it's much messier than it was. She begins to "rant and rave." The 14-year-old can see that Mother is so angry that physical abuse (violence) is only minutes away, as has happened before many times.

Understanding That Many Different Problems Can Cause Family Violence

Behavioral Objective: Students will learn to understand that violence and abuse are found in many families and that there are a variety of problems sometimes interacting with each other that can cause an outbreak of violence.

Directed Lesson:

1. ***Establish the Need:*** Family violence can be as subtle as verbal "put-downs" or as overt as beating and shooting. Children in families where violence (and/or abuse) is present often feel that they are to blame for what is happening. It is important for young people to understand that violence and abuse are very complex situations that could have a variety of causes interacting at the same time; children themselves are not to blame for family violence. In order to reduce the chance for family violence to take hold or to eliminate it if present, students need to recognize what family violence is and how abuse occurs; what they can do to protect themselves and other family members from violence and abuse; and how to seek assistance in dealing with such problems. Awareness of the problem, its causes and ways to address it will permit young people to, perhaps, help their family. In addition, it will help them in the future as adults with their own families since they will know the need and skills to provide a loving, nurturing environment free of violence and abuse for their children.

2. ***Introduction:*** The teacher will engage the students in a discussion about family violence using these or other suitable questions:

   ▸ **What can be the causes for family violence? (List on the board.)**

   ▸ **What constitutes family violence? (List on the board as students respond.)**

   ▸ **Who is/are the perpetrator(s) of such violence? (List)**

   ▸ **Who is/are the victim(s)? (List.)**

   ▸ **Which types of violence could threaten the safety of family members? (List)**

   ▸ **How could young persons (maybe your age) protect themselves or other family members from harm in a family which is violent and/or abusive?** (List)

3. ***Identify the Skill Components:*** Write the following skill components on the board or on sentence strips.

   1. Analyze the behavior that is causing the violence.

   2. Consider possible reasons for the behavior.

3. Decide if it threatens your safety or that of other family members.

4. If no, observe if the behavior becomes more threatening.

5. Think how the family could reduce the violent behavior.

6. Discuss your thoughts with a responsible adult.

7. Plan a strategy.

8. If yes, think about options for providing safety and assistance.

9. Decide what to do or who to ask for help.

10. Follow through with your decision.

4. ***Model the Skill:*** The teacher will model the teacher in the following scenario and will ask one student to role play Gail:

> **Gail, a tenth grade student, seeks out her teacher to discuss a family matter which has her worried. She tells the teacher that her mother and father have serious arguments about money. Her father's job position was reduced in pay. Her mother had to go to work. She has to pay her fees for basketball and is worried that this will cause another argument and that the argument might turn physically violent. She really wants to stay on the basketball team because the coach said she has the talent to get a basketball scholarship to college.**

The teacher will help Gail to apply the skill components to solve the situation and find a way out.

5. ***Behavioral Rehearsal:***

A. *Selection:* The teacher will select four groups of students to role play the following scenarios:

B. *Role Play:* Students will role play and apply the skill components to the following family behaviors:

– Carl, 18 years old, has noticed that his twelve-year-old sister has changed from a happy child to a somber one and that she gets nervous around Uncle Bill and doesn't want to have him touch her or even be left alone in the same room. Uncle Bill has been living with the family for six months, since he got out of the Army.

– Rose is the middle child. She is an average student compared to her bright, talented older sister and younger brother. She is very sweet, lovable, and kind, but not as smart or talented. Rose is tired of the verbal abuse from her siblings and parents that she's dumb, can't do anything, and will never amount to much.

– Jerry's older brother Fred always beats on him when something goes wrong, like the time when he got kicked off the football team. Fred beat him then, and Jerry was sore for several days. Fred has warned Jerry that he'd better not tell their parents or else he'll really get it. But Jerry is tired of being a punching bag.

– Elaine's mom and dad have always fought, and her mom usually ends up with bruises. Tonight is especially bad. When Elaine hears her dad say that he's going to get his gun and will make her mother stop making his life miserable, she feels really worried.

C. *Completion:* The teacher and class will determine if each role play is done correctly, reinforce correct behaviors, identify inappropriate behaviors and re-enact role play with correction, if necessary. If no corrections are needed, role play is complete.

D. *Reinforcers:* Verbal praise and/or applause will show appreciation for the efforts of the role playing students.

E. *Discussion:* The teacher will ask the following questions to help stimulate more discussion about violence in families. (Students should be asked to tell about violence in families without identifying the family whose violence they are describing.)

▶ **Was it easy or difficult for the youngsters in the role plays to deal with the behavior in their situations? Why?**

▶ **Can a family be exhibiting violent behaviors and yet no one in the family realizes that it is a violent family? How can that happen?**

▶ **Who is to blame for violence in families? Is it easy to identify any one person?**

▶ **Is it difficult for a family to accept that there is a problem of a violent nature within the family? Why?**

▶ **What do you think should be done to help families to be less violent and/or abusive?**

6. ***Practice:*** Distribute copies of the worksheet "What to Do!" for students to complete in class. When all students are done, ask them to share their answers.

7. ***Independent Use:*** The teacher will ask students to collect several newspaper or magazine articles which focus on an incident of family violence and bring them to class in one week. At that time, the teacher will have students discuss the stories of family violence to determine how the use of the skill components could have helped to solve any or all situations.

8. ***Continuation:*** The teacher will emphasize that students should know that family violence can and does occur in families regardless of socio-economic conditions, geographic location, religious affiliation, and so on. Children who experience violence in their families must understand that this is not how it should be, and that when they become adults having their own family, they should choose to reject violence as part of their family's lifestyle. However, until that time, this skill can help them to cope at present, and, as they grow up, to look forward to achieving a more peaceful lifestyle.

Name _____ Date _____

WHAT TO DO!

Directions: Describe ten (10) different behaviors of family violence and the cause that you think could have sparked each behavior. Then give your suggestions as to how these behaviors could have been curbed and prevented and what else you could have done. Use the skill components.

Family Violence **(Describe Between Whom)**	**Possible Cause(s)**	**What to Do!**

1. _____

2. _____

3. _____

4. _____

5. _____

6. _____

7. _____

8. _____

9. _____

10. _____

Recognizing Troublesome Situations

Behavioral Objective: Students will learn how to recognize situations that could potentially result in trouble and avoid them before they become explosive.

Directed Lessons:

1. **Establish the Need:** Young people often become involved in violent situations because they do not know how to recognize and leave incidents that potentially might lead to violence, even when they "see it coming." Students need to understand how to avoid possible problem situations by learning what they can do when they recognize that the situations could become violent, and how to act appropriately.

2. **Introduction:** The teacher will discuss the following items:

   - The typical places where young people often congregate.
   - The problems that can occur in such places.
   - How to recognize potentially violent situations.
   - What students can do under these conditions to avoid violence.

3. **Identify the Skill Components:** List the following skill components on the board or on sentence strips:

   1. Assess the situation.
   2. Identify the consequences of being a part of it.
   3. Consider your alternatives in order not to be involved.
   4. Consider removing yourself.
   5. Leave graciously, if you decide to do so.
   6. Make the best plan.
   7. Exercise your plan.

4. **Model the Skill:** The teacher will describe a time where he/she avoided a situation that he/she suspected in advance would be a problem. The teacher will use the skill components to explain why and how he/she avoided the problem and the benefits of doing so. An example the teacher might use is as follows:

   - Two teachers, both friends and peers of him/her, were arguing aggressively with each other in loud voices and asked him/her to decide who was right.

5. *Behavioral Rehearsal:*

A. *Selection:* The teacher will select three students who will each role play a personal experience that led to trouble.

B. *Role Play:* Each student will role play a difficult situation that occurred to him/her and show how he/she could have avoided the situation by utilizing the skill components.

C. *Completion:* After each role play, the teacher should reinforce the correct behavior and identify inappropriate behaviors. The students should repeat the role play with the new corrections if necessary. If it was well done and correct, the role play is complete.

D. *Reinforcers:* The class and teacher should applaud all role plays. Verbal and non-verbal praise from both the teacher and the class is essential.

E. *Discussion:* The teacher will lead the class in discussing how useful the skill components could be when encountering a situation that could become explosive.

6. *Practice:* The teacher will ask the students to complete the worksheet "I'm Out of Here!" and discuss it during class.

7. *Independent Use:* The teacher will distribute the worksheet "Double Trouble" for students to complete as a homework assignment and return in one week for discussion in class.

8. *Continuation:* The teacher will use appropriate experiences of trouble situations to discuss with the students how to spot dangerous and violent incidents in the future and how to avoid getting caught in them. He/she will emphasize the use of the skill components.

Name _____ Date _____

I'M OUT OF HERE!

Directions: In the space below, describe two situations where you avoided trouble by removing yourself from it.

1.

2.

Explain which skill components were used in these two situations.

1.

2.

Name _____ Date _____

DOUBLE TROUBLE

Directions: Complete the following paragraph in the space below.

I remember when I got in double trouble! I was already in enough trouble for being where I was not supposed to be, but then this happened on top of it. It all started when. . . .

Describe how you did solve the situation by using the skill components.

Reacting to Extremely Stressful Situations

Behavioral Objective: Students will be able to assess their individual stress levels, identify stressors, and react to extremely stressful situations in a reasonable and positive manner.

Directed Lesson:

1. **Establish the Need:** Today's sources of stress among teens are greater than in any other period in history. Family structure, family mobility, alienations, peer pressure, economics, and social conditions impact heavily on young people. As a result, some seek "quick fixes" and short-term solutions—even of a violent nature.

2. **Introduction:** The teacher will tell the following story:

   It was a usual English class on Friday the 13th. Mrs. Ellington, the teacher, asked her tenth grade composition class to write a set of three paragraphs related to "life." One of the class members, Margaret, seemed to be very pensive at the beginning of the assignment. As Mrs. Ellington circulated among the class members, she stopped and urged Margaret to get busy because time was fleeting and the paragraphs were due at the end of the period. As she spoke with Margaret, who had been absent from class for three days before, she noticed that Margaret had scribbled some statements on a scrap of paper. They were "I'm no good," "Everyone would be better off without me," and "If any thing happens to me." She then moved on to other students in the class.

   As the bell rang to signify the end of the last period of the day, Margaret was the first to turn in her paper and to leave the class.

   During the weekend, on Sunday evening, as Mrs. Ellington graded papers, she read what Margaret had written. It was a poem about death. The first line was "Everyone would be better off without me" and the last was "Good-bye Goodbye."

   The next day, as Mrs. Ellington picked up the small town Monday morning paper, she noticed an article about a teenager having a "serious accident." It did not give the name of the minor (under 18) involved. Later that morning she checked Margaret's homeroom and learned that Margaret was not in school. Then the principal called her to the office to inform her and Margaret's other teachers that Margaret had been hospitalized. There was much talk among the students about Margaret's problems at home related to the potential separation of her parents.

3. **Identify the Skill Components:** Write the following skill components on the board or on sentence strips:

1. Identify those situations that overstress you.

2. Identify why they overstress you.

3. Consider different means and activities to minimize the stress.

4. Consider the consequences of taking part in such activities.

5. Use means and activities that pose no serious or criminal consequences.

6. Decide if you have the ability to deal with the stress situation alone.

7. If not, seek assistance from a trusted adult.

8. Take a rational course of action.

4. ***Model the Skill:*** The teacher will share a stressful situation that occurred in dealing with a student(s) during his/her career. He/she will explain what considerations were given in handling the situation and what final course of action was taken. The teacher will emphasize those skill components that were applied.

5. ***Behavioral Rehearsal:***

   A. *Selection:* The teacher will select four pairs of students to play Margaret and Mrs. Ellington from the story in the introduction.

   B. *Role Play:* The teacher will ask the students to think of the story in the introduction and will suggest that Mrs. Ellington, the teacher in the story, might have realized (at the end of the first paragraph) that Margaret has problems. Each pair of students will play Margaret and Mrs. Ellington with Margaret having different stress problems, such as:

   (a) The parents are in the process of getting a divorce.

   (b) She is in love with a "no good" boy.

   (c) She is pregnant.

   (d) Her dog has just died.

   The student who plays Mrs. Ellington can either use the skill components to help Margaret or try to make Margaret use the skill components herself to find a way to deal with her stress in a positive way.

   C. *Completion:* After the role play, the teacher will highlight the correct responses, correct errors, and have students redo the role play, as necessary. If there are no corrections, the role play is complete.

   D. *Reinforcers:* The teacher and peers will thank students for appropriately completing the role play using the skill components. The class will identify the best role play and provide special compliments/recognition to the participants for their efforts.

   E. *Discussion:* The class will discuss and identify potential situations that cause extreme stress, especially in the life of a teenager, and list these situations on the board. The teacher will ask the students to copy this list of situations since they will use the list for their "practice" assignment.

6. ***Practice:*** Distribute copies of the worksheet entitled "Rx for Coping" for students to complete and discuss in class.

7. ***Independent Use:*** Hand out copies of the worksheet "Stress" for students to complete at home and return in one week for class discussion.

8. ***Continuation:*** The teacher will emphasize that everyone, from time to time, will have problems in life when extreme stresses are put on them. Therefore, it is most important to learn how to deal with such stresses and make sure that the means or activities used to reduce the stress have no serious consequences for them or their loved ones. Using this skill, students will know that they are in command and can cope with any stress without contemplating suicide.

Name _____ Date _____

R_x FOR COPING

This activity will help you develop a personal plan for coping with extreme stress in your life.

Directions: Select two causes of stress from the list that the class made earlier. Choose two that parallel your own experience and suggest five different strategies you could use to help you cope with each stress. Use the skill components if they are applicable and helpful.

Situation Causing Extreme Stress   **Coping Strategies**

#1

1. _____

2. _____

3. _____

4. _____

5. _____

#2

1. _____

2. _____

3. _____

4. _____

5. _____

Explain which of the skill components you used in each case and why they did help you to cope with the stress situation.

Name _____ Date _____

STRESS

Directions: Write a description of a highly stressful situation you saw on a television program or interview someone who has witnessed a highly stressful situation. Following either of these activities, complete the following.

1. Describe the situation.

2. How did the stressed person(s) react?

   – What were some thoughts the person(s) had?

   – How did the person(s) behave?
     A. rationally
     B. irrationally

   – Did they seek help?

   – Was help asked for?

   – Whom did they ask for help?

   – What type of help was provided?

   – Were there any consequences?

3. Were skill components applied to help in coping with the stress? Which?

4. How would you have reacted in a similar situation?

5. Would the skill components in this lesson have helped you to cope better with this situation? How?

Dealing with Dangerous Situations

Behavioral Objective: Students will learn to deal with dangerous situations when they are confronted by one or more persons threatening them with a weapon (gun, knife, etc.) in a way which allows them to diffuse the threat without the occurrence of violence.

Directed Lesson:

1. **Establish the Need:** Whether wanted for play, to get revenge, or to commit a crime, guns and other weapons are easily acquired by today's youth. Any situation where a gun or other weapon is involved can turn violent and deadly in a split second. According to statistics, youngsters are often threatened with a gun by peers and others. Therefore they need to learn to think and to act fast in such situations in order to avoid a violent outcome.

2. **Introduction:** The teacher will read the following story to the class.

   Carey is seventeen years old. She does a lot of babysitting to earn money. Carey is baby sitting for a new family on the block for the first time. As instructed she has put the children to bed by 9:30 P.M.—a boy seven, a girl nine, and the older boy eleven. A short time later, Carey looks up to see the eleven-year-old boy standing in the doorway waving a handgun and saying, "Look what I found!"

   The teacher asks the following questions to facilitate discussion of this dangerous situation involving a weapon.

   ▶ **Why is this a dangerous situation?**

   ▶ **How can it be diffused?**

   ▶ **What should Carey say to the parents when they get home?**

3. **Identify the Skill Components:** Write the following skill components on the board or on sentence strips:

   1. Recognize the seriousness of the situation.

   2. React quickly but calmly.

   3. Consider steps needed to stay safe.

   4. Diffuse the situation by doing some or all of the following:
      a. Use conversation.
      b. Do what is asked of you.
      c. Scream, yell for help.
      d. Get away, if possible.
      e. Call 911 or police.

   5. Report the incident immediately.

113

4. ***Model the Skill:*** The teacher will model how to use the skill components in the following situation to arrive at a peaceful solution.

   – The teacher is on hall duty before classes begin. He/she notices that two students are standing around one student who has a backpack partially open. The teacher sees a gun flash out and rapidly put back into the backpack.

5. ***Behavioral Rehearsal:***

   A. *Selection:* The teacher selects three pairs of students.

   B. *Role Play:* Each pair will role play one of the following dangerous situations:

      – You are upstairs with another family member studying when you hear what sounds like a gun shot coming from downstairs.

      – You are on a school bus when one of the students in the seat across from you takes a large hunting knife from a backpack and starts tossing it into the air.

      – You are walking down the street alone when you see a boy/girl from school. He/she approaches you, pulls out a gun, and says that he/she heard you have been "seeing" his/her girlfriend/boyfriend.

   C. *Completion:* After each group presents its role play, the teacher and remaining class members will determine if the skill components were used properly. If not, the teacher will identify the changes needed and ask the students to re-enact the role play with corrections. If there are no corrections, role play is complete.

   D. *Reinforcers:* Applause, a "thank you" from the teacher, and other positive reinforcement will acknowledge the cooperation and participation of the role playing students.

   E. *Discussion:* Each group will discuss their role play explaining how and why they diffused the situation and what the danger is in dealing with such situations. The teacher might ask if anyone has personally experienced such a situation and how they dealt with it at the time. These personal experiences could be used for future role plays to provide additional practice of the skill.

6. ***Practice:*** The teacher will ask the students to complete the worksheet "Dangerous Situations" and call upon them to share their responses with the class.

7. ***Independent Use:*** The teacher will give students copies of the worksheet "Ways to Respond" and ask them to complete it outside of class and return it at a designated time to discuss in class.

8. ***Continuation:*** The teacher will tell the students that some situations may be very difficult to diffuse. The only way to protect themselves in such situations is to cooperate, stay calm, think fast, and consider various options. By doing so, they may be able to reduce the danger or even get through it unharmed. The teacher will remind students that it is important to report such occurrences to the proper authorities (or parents) in order to lessen the chances for such situations to happen again, thus helping to reduce and/or eliminate some of the violence that plagues our country and the world.

Name _____ Date _____

DANGEROUS SITUATIONS

Directions: Describe how you would resolve the following three situations in a safe manner based on using the skill components. Use the bottom half of the page to explain how you would do this; use the back of the page if necessary.

Situation 1:

Mark has been hassling you for weeks on your way to school each day. He already has your best jacket, lunch money, and your favorite gold chain and ring. Yet he still continues to hassle you. You have decided that he's not going to hassle you any longer and tell him so when he approaches you the next day. He tells you that this isn't a smart thing to say and pulls out a gun.

Situation 2:

Your best friend Shannon's life has been a mess. She hasn't been sleeping well, is edgy, and seems to have something negative to say about everybody. After school one day, she shows you a pistol she bought for $15.00 from Marco on the street. She tells you that now everyone will know who's in charge.

Situation 3:

It's the State Championship against your school's biggest rival. While watching the game, you look behind you and see a boy opening his gym bag. "This is for after the game, just in case there's any trouble," he tells his friends, as he shows them the 9mm that he has inside.

Name _____ Date _____

WAYS TO RESPOND

Directions: List 5 dangerous situations that you might encounter in your life and tell how you would safely diffuse the situations.

The Dangerous Situation	Strategies to Diffuse the Dangerous Situation Safely

Managing Threatening Situations

Behavioral Objective: Students will learn how to manage threatening situations and to deal with dangerous individuals in the neighborhood of their home and school by using decision-making strategies.

Directed Lesson:

1. **Establish the Need:** Students need to feel empowered to manage threatening situations by learning to recognize the possible dangers that are present when confronted with any of those situations. Students may also learn how to deal with persons in their school or neighborhood who seem to be acting in an unusual or strange manner which they think could create and inflate a threatening situation. Students will be better prepared to deal with such situations if they use good decision-making skills and know how and whom to ask for help.

2. **Introduction:** The teacher will ask the students to respond to the following questions:

   ▶ **What would you do if someone offered to give you a ride?**

   ▶ **What would you do if someone offered you a drink from an opened bottle in a brown paper bag?**

   ▶ **What would you do if you saw a person you do not know standing in front of your house, acting in an unusual or strange manner?**

   ▶ **What would you do if a student on the school bus started passing around a hunting knife?**

   The teacher will offer the following as possible resources to ask for help:

   Block Watch . . . Call 911 . . . Police . . . Teacher . . . Counselor . . . Minister . . . Neighbor . . . Parent

3. **Identify the Skill Components:** Write the following skill components on the board or on sentence strips:

   1. Observe carefully what is happening around you.
   2. Decide if a dangerous situation is imminent.
   3. If yes, decide which safety measures should be taken.
   4. If a person is the cause for concern, decide if he/she needs help.
   5. Consider if you need help.
   6. Consider who could provide the best help.
   7. Do what is needed to get help.
   8. Decide if action is required, such as leaving the scene.
   9. Do what provides the greatest safety.

117

4. ***Model the Skill:*** The teacher will model how to use the skill components in the following story: He/she is home alone. It is about 10:30 PM. It is difficult for him/her to walk because of recent foot surgery. He/she notices that a flashlight is being pointed at the living room window, then at the kitchen window.

Using a "think aloud" approach, the teacher will manage the situation and show how the skill components help in the situation.

5. ***Behavioral Rehearsal:***

   A. *Selection:* The teacher will select two pairs of students and a single student to role play.

   B. *Role Play:* The teacher will ask the students to role play the following situations. (These scenes can be written on index cards or explained verbally to the role players.)

      – The person who drove you to a party becomes very drunk.

      – You are approached by another student and asked if you want to see his dad's gun which he has in his backpack.

      – While you are at the mall, you notice that a man has been following you for the last 40 minutes and is still behind you.

   C. *Completion:* After each role play, the teacher will decide if the role play was done correctly and if the skill components were used appropriately. If corrections are needed, the role plays will be re-enacted; if not, the role play is complete.

   D. *Reinforcers:* The teacher and class will thank the role players for their participation with applause and verbal remarks.

   E. *Discussion:* The teacher will ask the class the following questions:

      ▶ **How did the skill components help in each of the role plays?**

      ▶ **Have you ever been in a similar situation?**

      ▶ **If anything similar happened to you, how could the skill components be of benefit to you?**

      ▶ **Whom would you ask for help?**

6. ***Practice:*** Distribute the worksheet "Situations" for students to complete in class. After they have completed it, have students share their responses.

7. ***Independent Use:*** Hand out copies of the worksheet "Help." Ask the students to complete the worksheet at home and bring it back in one week to discuss in class.

8. ***Continuation:*** The teacher will emphasize the importance of managing dangerous situations and knowing when and whom to ask for help. The teacher will indicate also that managing dangerous situations requires us to make the right decisions in a moment's time.

Name _____ Date _____

SITUATIONS

Directions: Think of two examples of situations when you had to use decision-making skills to avoid danger. Describe, using full paragraphs, how you solved the problem then and how you would solve it now using the skill components.

Situation #1 (describe briefly)

What did you do then to be safe?

What will you do now in a similar situation knowing the skill components?

Did you ask for help? Whom did you ask?

Was the response different then and now? Why?

Did the use of the skill components help in the decision-making process? Why?

Situation #2 (describe briefly)

What did you do then to be safe?

What would you do now in a similar situation knowing the skill components?

Did you ask for help? Whom did you ask?

Was the response different then and now? Why?

Did the use of the skill components help in the decision-making process? Why?

Name _____ Date _____

HELP

Directions: Find a news story in the newspaper or from the TV that has a sad ending but could have ended well if the person(s) had been aware of the danger and known how to act to prevent the sad consequences. Describe the story as it happened and how it could have had a better ending if the person(s) involved had been alert and aware that there was danger around. Do not forget to describe in detail how the danger could have been noticed and what could have been done to avert it.

Coping with Excessive Stress

Behavioral Objective: Students will learn how to cope with stress caused by excessive pressure created by their own ambitions or those of others (parents, coaches, etc.) to achieve at levels more than possible for them.

Directed Lessons:

1. **Establish the Need:** In some people, the drive to excel or be noticed in some way is so strong that they push themselves constantly to go "above and beyond." Youngsters, too, can put excessive pressure on themselves to succeed or others, such as parents, exert pressure on children to achieve the highest grades, be accepted into the best schools, and excel in a multitude of activities. Sometimes the student does not possess the desire, ability, and/or talent to achieve at the expected levels; then, this pressure can have detrimental effects on the student's well-being and health to the point where the pressure becomes so intolerable that the student collapses, has a nervous breakdown, or even commits suicide. Students need to be able to judge when unrealistically high expectations or demands are causing excessive stress and should understand how to modify their activities and participation to reduce the pressure.

2. **Introduction:** The teacher will read the following story to the class:

   Paul is a sophomore who is being pressured by his mother to follow in his grandfather's footsteps. Her late father had a glowing career which earned him a Nobel Prize in Physics. Since Paul is her only child, she wants him to excel in math and science as did his grandfather. Although Paul has some aptitude for math and science, he is more interested in sports and would like to prepare for a business career in the sports field. He also enjoys the physical competition of sports such as track, basketball, and football.

   Paul tries to please his mother, but his math and science grades are never "good enough" for his mother. He is beginning to experience severe headaches whenever she talks about a career in physics or when he is working on the math and science assignments. His friends are encouraging him to try out for track and football, which he would really like to do; but his mother says if he spent more time studying science he could get better grades.

   The teacher will pose the following questions:

   ▶ **Who is putting pressure on Paul?**

   ▶ **If he rejects his mother's plans for him, is he saying he doesn't love her? Explain.**

> ▶ **How can he best handle the pressure?**
> ▶ **If you were Paul, what would you do?**

3. ***Identify the Skill Components:*** Write the following skill components on the board or on sentence strips:

   1. Determine if you are excessively stressed.
   2. Analyze who puts the pressure upon you.
   3. Decide your own limitations.
   4. Define what you can and cannot do.
   5. Discuss your limitations with those exerting pressure.
   6. Limit your activities.
   7. Postpone some activities to a later time.
   8. Make a plan to reduce the stress.
   9. Re-evaluate the plan as needed.

4. ***Model the Skill:*** The teacher will share a personal experience where he/she was pressured to excel at a level beyond his/her capability. The teacher will use the skill components to show how to react to excessive stress.

5. ***Behavioral Rehearsal:***

   A. *Selection:* The teacher will select two pairs of students to role play.

   B. *Role Play:* The two pairs of students will role play the following scenarios:

   One pair of students will role play the story of Paul from the introduction, showing how Paul can use the skill components for making a plan to relieve the stress put upon him by his mother. One student will role play Paul and the other his mother.

   The second pair of students will role play the following story:

   > **The whole class decided, by majority vote, to participate in a marathon which was arranged for a charitable purpose. One student of the pair will refuse to participate in the marathon while the other one will pressure him/her to join in the running. Using the skill components will help the student to plan how to get out of the running, knowing that it is physically too strenuous and considering his/her condition of health.**

   Other role plays can be suggested by students or the teacher, as time permits.

6. ***Practice:*** The teacher will distribute copies of the worksheet "Under Pressure" to be completed in class and discussed after completion.

7. ***Independent Use:*** The teacher will hand out the worksheet "Excessive Stress" and ask the students to complete and return it in one week for discussion in class.

8. ***Continuation:*** The teacher will point out that mastering this skill is useful whenever students experience pressure to perform beyond their limits of capability and interest. It can help them to evaluate why they are being pressured, and by whom, their ability to comply, and how to respond in a way that is in their best interest.

Name _____ Date _____

 # UNDER PRESSURE

Directions: Describe how you would respond if you were faced with the following situations.

Situation A You injured your leg before the big game. Your parents and coach want you to play because some college scouts may be there. Are you going to play basketball?

   1. Describe what you will do.

   2. How can the skill components be helpful in making a decision?

Situation B You studied very hard and got a B on your final exam. Your mother isn't satisfied and wants you to take it over. What do you say to Mom?

   1. Describe what you will do.

   2. How can the skill components be helpful in planning your decision?

Situation C You're not allowed to discontinue your piano lessons even though your fingers cramp a lot when playing. Whom do you talk to?

   1. Describe what you will do.

   2. How can the skill components be helpful in making this decision?

Name _____ Date _____

EXCESSIVE STRESS

Directions: Write a story about a young person experiencing excessive stress to excel beyond his/her ability. Describe the situation, who is applying pressure, how it is affecting the young person, and how the young person deals with it. Before returning the worksheet to class for discussion, share it with your parents at home and have one of your parents sign it.

Parent _____

Learning to Trust Others

Behavioral Objective: Students will learn that it is important to trust and to communicate with others when under stress due to difficulties, which to them seem not resolvable.

Directed Lesson:

1. **Establish the Need:** In today's self-centered environment, youth may feel that no one cares and that they cannot trust anyone. Feeling alone and helpless can undermine feelings of self-worth and can create such strong feelings of rejection and depression that suicide is considered the only solution for salvation. Youth need to understand that it is most important to have someone they can trust, to confide in, communicate with, and ask for assistance when they find themselves in stressful and/or dangerous situations which might create feelings of self-doubt and even lead to suicide.

2. **Introduction:** The teacher will share the following story with the students:

   John/Jean is a middle/high school student. He/She is a good student and a successful athlete. Recently, he/she has had a major problem with her/his boyfriend/girlfriend and they haven't seen each other for a month. The teachers are concerned that her/his grades have dropped and the coach has benched her/him due to several poor performances. The student's parents want an explanation for this sudden change. The teachers, coach, and parents are claiming that a lack of effort and poor attitude are at fault. John/Jean feels confused, helpless, and all alone. In fact, on several occasions, John/Jean has said that things would be better if he/she was dead.

   The teacher then asks the following questions:

   ▶ **How has John/Jean come to such a point in his/her young life that being dead seems to be the best solution?**

   ▶ **How can this situation be resolved without harm to anyone?**

   ▶ **Would it help John/Jean to have someone in whom he/she could confide? Why?**

   ▶ **How could John/Jean find someone to trust? What characteristics should this person possess?**

   ▶ **Name some professional people who could be considered.**

3. **Identify the Skill Components:** Write the following skill components on the board or on sentence strips:

   1. Define the characteristics a trusted person should have.

   2. Select someone who meets your criteria.

3. Communicate clearly and honestly.

4. Listen to what is said by you and others.

5. Determine why you are stressed or depressed.

6. Decide how to safely resolve the problem.

7. Follow through to resolve the problem.

8. Remember that more than one attempt may be needed.

9. Acknowledge your feelings of relief.

4. *Model the Skill:* Using the story from the introduction, the teacher will portray John/Jean and role play how employing the skill components could improve the situation for John/Jean. A student may be asked by the teacher to assist him/her by role playing the trusted person.

5. *Behavioral Rehearsal:*

A. *Selection:* The teacher will select as many pairs of students to role play as time permits.

B. *Role Play:* One student in each pair of students will role play the stressed/depressed person and the other will be the trusted person. The following four situations can be used, or the teacher may make up his/her own or use experiences suggested by the students.

   – Sheridan is under tremendous pressure from his parents to be an A+ student in all subjects, to maintain his leadership position on the swimming team, and to keep a job to help pay for his own clothes, etc. Sheridan is always tired and misses just "hanging out" with friends.

   – Mary is very lonely. She is new at this school and is having difficulty making new friends. She misses her old neighborhood and friends so much that she cries a lot and doesn't even feel like eating.

   – Alonzo is being threatened to join a gang or suffer the consequences. He really doesn't want to join because in the last year, three members have been shot by rival gangs and one died as a result. Yet, Alonzo knows that the "consequences" of not joining means a severe beating.

   – Cherie has just learned that she has leukemia and will have to undergo extensive chemotherapy. There is no guarantee that the disease can be controlled and she knows that the chemo will make her sick and cause her to temporarily lose her hair, which is very lovely, wavy, thick, shiny, black hair. (Her dad always calls her his "beautiful raven.") She is so depressed that she told her parents that she wishes she were dead now so that she would not have to go through all that is ahead of her.

C. *Completion:* The teacher and class will determine if the role play was done correctly and if the skill components were used in the role play. If necessary, the role play will be re-enacted with corrections; if there are no corrections, the role play is complete.

D. *Reinforcers:* The teacher will thank the role playing students for their excellent ideas in assisting their friends in solving some very difficult situations of depression.

E. *Discussion:* The teacher will ask the students the following questions:

▶ **How can talking with a trusted person help in, what seems, a desperate situation?**

▶ **Why would thinking about suicide as the answer to one's problem be the worst possible choice?**

▶ **If you knew some persons who were stressed or depressed, what would you do to help them?**

▶ **Would anyone like to share an example of a situation when they needed to talk to someone trusted about a serious problem and describe how the person assisted?**

6. ***Practice:*** The teacher will distribute and ask the students to complete the worksheet "Search for Trust" as a follow-up to the skill discussed in today's lesson.

7. ***Independent Use:*** The teacher will ask the students to complete the "Interview" worksheet at home and return it in one week to share in class.

8. ***Continuation:*** The teacher will emphasize that most people need a trusted person at some time during their life. Students should realize that being able to communicate with someone you trust can be very beneficial in solving difficult problems and maintaining good mental attitude.

Name _____ Date _____

 SEARCH FOR TRUST

Directions: Find these words. They can be left to right, right to left, top to bottom, bottom to top, or on diagonals.

DEPRESSED	COMMUNICATE	FRIENDS
HEALTH	TRUST	STRESS
DECIDE	LISTEN	MENTAL
FEELINGS	RELIEF	TALK
HELP	ASK	SUCCESS

M	E	N	T	A	L	I	S	T	E	N
A	T	C	Q	E	H	E	A	L	T	H
F	A	D	S	U	C	C	E	S	S	F
E	C	E	D	M	T	R	G	V	R	L
E	I	C	P	F	R	I	E	N	D	S
L	N	I	L	X	U	K	X	O	U	S
I	U	D	E	J	S	S	E	P	K	E
N	M	E	H	Z	T	D	P	W	S	R
G	M	L	N	C	I	X	K	L	A	T
S	O	R	E	L	I	E	F	M	Q	S
B	C	D	E	P	R	E	S	S	E	D

SEARCH FOR TRUST
Answer Key

M	E	N	T	A	L	I	S	T	E	N
A	T	C	Q	E	H	E	A	L	T	H
F	A	D	S	U	C	C	E	S	S	F
E	C	E	D	M	T	R	G	V	R	L
E	I	C	P	F	R	I	E	N	D	S
L	N	I	L	X	U	K	X	O	U	S
I	U	D	E	J	S	S	E	P	K	E
N	M	E	H	Z	T	D	P	W	S	R
G	M	L	N	C	I	X	K	L	A	T
S	O	R	E	L	I	E	F	M	Q	S
B	C	D	E	P	R	E	S	S	E	D

Name _____   Date _____

INTERVIEW

Directions: Interview two adult family members about a time when they needed a trusted person to help them to solve a problem. Record the interview below.

Family Member	Relationship of trusted person?	Why did you choose to trust this person?	How did you feel after talking with this person?	Have you ever been the trusted person for someone?

Dealing with Deep Depressions

Behavioral Objective: Students will understand the need and importance to openly discuss feelings of depression, which might vent the idea of committing suicide, with adults in their lives and seek the comfort of getting help from adults.

Directed Lessons:

1. **Establish the Need:** Suicide among high school students is an ever-increasing threat to stability and safety within the school. The prevalence of drugs, weapons, and alcohol among teens often "masks" the depression that exists among the adolescent group. Increasingly, students do not seek the assistance of adults, but rather turn inward and to their "inexperienced" peers for assistance. Often, much of their concern is not shared and results in suicide. High school students, as their peers, often feel helpless and guilty for not being able to have influenced positively the outcome of events leading to the suicide of one of their friends, peers, or acquaintances. Youth need to understand the importance of open communications with others, especially adults, at all times.

2. **Introduction:** The teacher will read the following story, "Parody of Death," to students:

   The one room loft was deserted—a desolate open area that was cold, dark and uninhabited. The flashing neon light, from the bar below, reflected into the window. Chris sat on the floor in the corner with the wall stretching upward, seeming to go on forever. No one was around and the only sounds were of the cars rushing by on the street below. No one wanted to be with Chris, so to ease his loneliness, he pulled a can of beer out of the plastic rings and thrust his head back against the wall and swallowed most of the beer in one gulp. Chris felt the urge to drink often, but he never considered his drinking a problem. One beer was not enough. He pulled beer after beer out of the clear plastic casing and each one was the same. He did not drink for the taste or the pleasure. His only motive was to forget about the many troubles that he faced daily.

   Soon, the alcohol was not enough to repress his sadness and anger and he needed to do something more. In his mind, the dimensions of his problems grew larger and his depression became overwhelming. He remembered the packet that was given to him by his friend whom he had asked to provide him with a stimulant. It had been in his coat pocket since the previous evening when he had left the bar. His "friend" said that a small amount of the material in the packet would take him places that he had never been before. So he thought it was some kind of stimulant he had requested. The friend had told him to take only a small amount at a time. But he felt so desolate that he needed help and swallowed the

131

total amount in one gulp. Chris felt that this would help him to forget about his problems and loneliness and he would not be alone any more.

Only a few moments after he had consumed the total material contained in the package, the room was filled with colors. Everything was spinning and when the whirlwind ceased, there were people everywhere. Some were his friends from the past; others were his relatives. Some he had never seen before. He perceived the people whom he had never seen before as "gifts" who would become his salvation. One individual was rather peculiar looking to Chris. Dark circles encased his eyes, his hair was long and disheveled, he wore a black robe and carried a cane that had a skull perched on the end of it. The people were laughing, singing, dancing, and having a great time. Chris approached some of the guys and started talking. Soon his speech became slurred, his vision blurred and his pulse faint. He could no longer help himself. . . .

The teacher will ask the following questions:

- ▶ **What do you think brought this situation about?**
- ▶ **What would have helped Chris?**
- ▶ **Who could have helped Chris?**
- ▶ **After the incident, what did his classmates do?**

3. ***Identify the Skill Components:*** Write the following skill components on the board or on sentence strips:

1. Consider the reasons for your depression.

2. Recognize your symptoms of depression.

3. Analyze potential consequences of your depression.

4. Think of some legitimate means to overcome the depression.

5. Consider sharing your feelings with an adult.

6. Decide with whom to communicate.

7. Decide if a doctor's advice would be appropriate.

8. Follow the best course of action.

4. ***Model the Skill:*** The teacher will model the skill by using the skill components in a situation that the students are or were aware of, which involved a serious depression, and show how it can be overcome by finding legitimate means through discussion and interaction with adults. The situation might be:

- a college challenge

- the loss of a loved one

- the loss of a close colleague

5. ***Behavioral Rehearsal:***

A. *Selection:* The teacher will ask for three students who have had intimate knowledge of a suicide situation. Those three students will work, each with another student also selected by the teacher, to do three role plays.

132

B. *Role Play:* The students will role play the actual situations of each suicide known to one of the students in each group. The students will use the skill components to help them to arrive at solutions to the situations other than suicide, since any problem can be solved with good reasoning. (Names to be used should be fictitious.)

C. *Completion:* As each role play is finished, the teacher will determine if the role play was appropriate. If not, the teacher will ask the students to re-enact the role play with corrections. If yes, the role play is complete.

D. *Reinforcers:* Teacher and peers should acknowledge correct behavior with verbal praise. Special acknowledgment will be given to students who have learned to ask for help when needed.

E. *Discussion:* The teacher will start a discussion by asking the following questions:

- **Why do some people think about suicide and even do it?**
- **How can family and friends know that someone is considering suicide?**
- **Who do you think suffers the most in a case of suicide?**
- **Does suicide *really* solve a problem?**

6. *Practice:* Distribute copies of the worksheet "What, Who?" for students to complete and discuss it in class.

7. *Independent Use:* The teacher will distribute the "Interview Sheet" and will ask the students to use it to interview a school/community related support person (i.e., counselor, social worker, law enforcement officer, cleric, doctor, psychologist) to find out how they could help a person in despair in a given situation. The teacher will ask the students to complete the Interview Sheets and return them to class in one week for discussion. At that time, the teacher might want to have students prepare a large chart which describes the symptoms of depression and indicates what they and/or the support persons contacted by the students suggested to do in order to assist in overcoming the depression and assisting the person.

8. *Continuation:* The teacher will remind students often of the need to view "challenges as opportunities" and to communicate with adults when they feel "haunted" by a deep depression.

Name _____ Date _____

WHAT, WHO?

I. Directions: Describe in accordance with the table below five symptoms which indicate serious depression and what to do to overcome the depression.

Symptoms of Depression	Ways to Deal with the Symptoms	Whom Can You Get to Help?
1.		
2.		
3.		
4.		
5.		

II. Describe a perceived "overwhelming" situation that you have experienced and how it was successfully overcome. Then, identify the skill components related to the situation which were applied to overcome the challenge.

Situation:

List skill components applied in its solution:

III. List the "coping skills" you will use when challenged by difficult situations. How can these help you?

Name _____ Date _____

INTERVIEW SHEET

1. Describe an actual or made-up situation that caused the person's despair.

2. Describe the behavior and feelings of the person in despair (symptoms of depression).

3. Give the title and position of the person you interviewed for assistance:

4. Describe what the person you interviewed suggested to do.

5. Describe how the person you interviewed would assist the person in despair.

6. Describe what causes and symptoms the person in despair had, which you discussed with the support person and what was suggested to be done.

7. State your ideas about the assistance that was suggested and whether you think it was helpful and would help the person in despair.

8. State the suggestions you would have to assist the person in despair and why you think they would help.

Understanding the Danger of Addiction

Behavioral Objective: Students will learn that "trying" stimulants and other drugs might lead to addiction, which is difficult to conquer. Addiction means craving stimulants and requiring successively larger portions to satisfy the craving. This costs more and more money and can lead to serious consequences such as violence, crime, and suicide.

Directed Lesson:

1. ***Establish the Need:*** Too many young people commit suicide each year. In many cases, the use of a stimulant or other type of drug has contributed to or is directly responsible for their action. Although many youths believe that stimulants will help them "feel good" the actual results can be hallucinations, isolation, and depression, which can lead to suicide, either planned or accidental. Therefore, youth need to learn not to use stimulants for any reason, that even a first try can lead to addiction which is very difficult to conquer, and that professional treatment is the only approach to overcome such cravings.

2. ***Introduction:*** The teacher will ask the students to name some addictive stimulants (list on the board). The teacher will then explain that all stimulants are addictive in different degrees and that each person's threshold for addiction does vary. The teacher will next read the following story:

    Mike was a young college student and very bright. For extra money, he was a waiter at a restaurant. His co-workers at the restaurant where he was employed asked him to join them at a party. When he arrived he saw that cocaine was the main attraction at this party. He was quickly asked to join in; he said yes immediately because he had always wondered how cocaine makes a person feel and was curious to participate in the experience. He liked his reaction to cocaine and was almost immediately addicted.

    Mike did not live at home. He was able to keep his addiction a secret from his family. His roommate and girlfriend, who knew about his addiction, did not tell his parents. His girlfriend tried to convince him to get treatment for his addiction. He refused, telling her that he could stop any time he wanted and that he liked the way cocaine made him feel. As usually happens in cases of a stimulant addiction, the amount of cocaine needed to make Mike feel good kept increasing. He was becoming depressed when the cocaine effect wore off and, because he would not go for treatment, his girlfriend broke off their relationship.

    One evening, after a cocaine party, deep depression set in. Mike continued to party with a friend by finishing off a few cans of beer, hoping this would make him feel better. After the friend brought him home, he must have felt totally

depressed due to the combined effects of cocaine and alcohol. This probably caused him to think of suicide. All that is known is that his roommate found him in the morning, hanging from a tree in front of their apartment building.

Did Mike need help? What could he have done differently?

The teacher will ask the students to respond to the following additional questions:

- ▶ **What was the cause of Mike's suicide?**
- ▶ **Since Mike did not realize that he needed professional help, who could have helped him and how?**
- ▶ **How do you think his roommate and girlfriend feel?**
- ▶ **How do you think his parents feel?**
- ▶ **How will his suicide affect his parents, roommate, and girlfriend?**
- ▶ **Will there be lasting effects?**

3. *Identify the Skill Components:* Write the following skill components on the board or on sentence strips:

1. Know that all stimulants and most types of drugs are addictive.
2. Consider all the consequences of stimulant and other drug use.
3. Remember that one try can lead to addiction.
4. Resolve to yourself that you will not use drugs as stimulants.
5. If already using stimulants, realize that you will need help.
6. Remember that your life is important.
7. Remember that professional treatment is available.
8. Decide what to do.
9. Make a wise decision.

4. *Model the Skill:* The teacher will role play Mike from the story in the introduction after he had tried cocaine for the very first time. Using the skill components, the teacher will show how the outcome for Mike could have been different.

5. *Behavioral Rehearsal:*

A. *Selection:* The teacher will select 3 groups of 3 students, each including one boy to role play Mike, one boy to role play his roommate, and one girl to role play his girlfriend.

B. *Role Play:* In the role plays, Mike's roommate and his girlfriend will help Mike to deal with his problem. To do so they will make use of the skill components.

C. *Completion:* The teacher and class will decide if the role play was correct and if the skill components were used appropriately in each role play. If corrections are needed, the role play will be reenacted; if no corrections are needed, the role play is complete.

D. *Reinforcers:* A big thank you from the teacher will acknowledge the participation of the role playing students.

E. *Discussion:* The teacher will ask students the following questions:

> ▶ **What are the symptoms of stimulant use?**
> ▶ **Why do stimulants affect different people in different degrees?**
> ▶ **Can you tell before trying a stimulant to what degree it will affect you?**
> ▶ **What would be your best response to an offer to try a stimulant?**
> ▶ **What do you think you would do if one of your friends was using a stimulant?**
> ▶ **Would you want someone to help you if you were using a stimulant? How?**
> ▶ **How do you think the skill components will help you to make the right decision about stimulant use?**

6. ***Practice:*** Distribute copies of the worksheet "Good Friend" and ask students to write a story in which a good friend is the main character who becomes addicted to a stimulant. In the story, students will describe the addiction, how it is affecting the friend's life, who helps him/her deal with the problem, and how and what happens to the friend at the end of the story. Stories will be shared in class, as time permits.

7. ***Independent Use:*** The teacher will ask the students to work in groups of 3 or 4 to gather information about stimulants, addiction, and treatment. Each group will plan how to present the information they have gathered along with a poster with the theme of abstaining from the use of stimulants and any other drugs. The stories are due back in two weeks for discussion and the posters will then be placed around the room or in the hallway.

8. ***Continuation:*** The teacher will again emphasize that even a "first try" can lead to addiction and that buying, selling, or using stimulants by unauthorized persons is illegal and can lead to serious consequences. Students should be encouraged to make a commitment to themselves not to use, or even try, stimulants or other drugs. The teacher will remind the students that no problem is ever so great that it can't be solved. They can always find a positive way to do so, if they look hard enough and long enough.

Name _____ Date _____

GOOD FRIEND
(A Creative Story)

Understanding the Consequences of Taking Stimulants

Behavioral Objective: Students will learn that the use of drugs as stimulants can cloud their judgment and thus can make them vulnerable or more aggressive and even violent, for example, in their relationships with the opposite sex and also with peers of their own sex.

Directed Lessons:

1. **Establish the Need:** Young people need to learn to understand that using drugs as stimulants can cloud their judgment and actions and cause them, for example, to become unduly aggressive and even use violence. This type of behavior can become a serious problem when having an intimate relationship with the opposite gender since it can lead to unwanted sexual advances, violent reactions, sexually-transmitted diseases, unwanted pregnancy, AIDS, etc. Youth, therefore, need to learn that in order to keep control over their actions and to respect and cherish their relationships, they have to refrain from taking stimulants.

2. **Introduction:** The teacher will review the emotional and behavioral effects of using stimulants by asking students to name them. (Make a list on the board.) The teacher will then have the students respond to and discuss the following:

   ▶ **Why does the use of stimulants lead to violent behavior?**

   ▶ **Can it lead to unwanted sex?**

   ▶ **Can it end a good relationship?**

   ▶ **What can be the consequences of unwanted sex?**

   ▶ **Can either partner be a victim or perpetrator?**

   ▶ **How could it affect the life of each partner?**

3. **Identify the Skill Components:** Write the following skill components on the board or on sentence strips:

   1. Decide if a relationship is out of hand.

   2. Decide if stimulant or drug use is the reason.

   3. If yes, decide how to discontinue the use of stimulants.

   4. Define your role in the relationship.

   5. Consider all consequences.

   6. Decide how you want this relationship to be changed.

   7. Consider what you can do to effect this change.

   8. Consider if you should end the relationship.

   9. Do what is best for you.

4. ***Model the Skill:*** The teacher will model the skill by modeling the role of a teen who is at a party with her boyfriend. He has been drinking and is making very rude sexual remarks to her. He is trying to grab and fondle her. She goes to the bathroom to get away for a few minutes. She doesn't like how he is acting and is considering how to get out of the situation. The teacher, role playing her, shows the class what to do by using the skill components. The teacher could ask a student to role play the boyfriend.

5. ***Behavioral Rehearsal:***

   A. *Selection:* The teacher will select three groups of two and three students to role play the following scenarios:

   B. *Role Play:* The teacher will ask the selected students to role play the following situations which have been written on index cards by the teacher.

      – After having a few drinks, Devon keeps pressuring Annette to have sex with him. He says that if she really loves him, she would. Devon is always trying to get Annette to drink more beer and liquor than she thinks she can handle. Annette talks about that to her very best friend, Crystal.

      – Paul, Carl and Patrick (Paula, Carla and Patricia) are good friends. They like to do things together. One day they went together to a picnic and two of them had some beer, while one of them refused to drink. It did not take long before the two drinking partners became boisterous and both attacked their non-drinking friend for not joining them in having "fun." This all ended in a bitter fight. All three got hurt. The next day all three discuss what to do to prevent another fight.

      – Carol, Mary, and Sue are having a sleep over at Carol's house. Mary has a short sleeveless nightgown on, which reveals to the other two girls some old bruises on Mary's upper arms and thighs along with one really bad bruise on her arm. When they ask her how she got them, she reluctantly tells them that sometimes when her boyfriend gets "high" and they are being intimate, he gets very mean and usually breaks off the intimacy and just beats on her. Carol and Sue try to discuss with Mary how she could prevent that from happening again.

   C. *Completion:* The teacher and class will analyze the role play and the use of the skill components. If corrections are needed, the teacher will ask students to re-enact the role play. Otherwise, the role play is complete.

   D. *Reinforcers:* Compliments and applause from the teacher and students will acknowledge the efforts of the role players.

   E. *Discussion:* The teacher will lead the discussion with the following questions:

      ▶ **Do you know of anyone who was in a situation similar to those in the role plays?**

      ▶ **How do you think the victim feels in such situations?**

      ▶ **How do you think the perpetrator feels toward the victim?**

      ▶ **How could the skill components help to mitigate such situations?**

6. ***Practice:*** The teacher will distribute the worksheet "Unwanted Situations" to the students to be completed in class and discussed.

7. ***Independent Use:*** The teacher will ask the students to design a cartoon strip at home with words on the balloons to demonstrate the concept of this skill and remind students to show how teenage boys and girls can use the skill components to avoid the use of stimulants, such as alcohol, inhalants, and drugs, in order to prevent the likelihood of an assaultive and violent situation. The teacher requests that the students bring the cartoon strip to class in one week for discussion in the class.

8. ***Continuation:*** The teacher will emphasize that situations similar to those in the role plays can happen to anyone, male or female, and can occur at home, at school, in the neighborhood or at any other place. Students must remember that the use of stimulants, even when taken for the purpose of experimentation, can have serious and violent consequences.

Name _____ Date _____

"UNWANTED SITUATIONS"

Directions: Identify three circumstances which could put you in an unwanted sexual situation. Describe each situation—where, when, with whom. Tell what you would do to get out of the situation and how you could use the skill components to take control of the situation.

1. Describe the situation:

   TAKE CONTROL:

2. Describe the situation:

   TAKE CONTROL:

3. Describe the situation:

   TAKE CONTROL:

Maintaining Rational Thinking

Behavioral Objective: Students will learn that stimulants such as alcohol, cigarettes, marijuana, etc. can impair the ability to think and behave rationally and thus to understand fully the intentions of others.

Directed Lesson:

1. **Establish the Need:** Young people often believe the use of stimulants, such as alcohol, will improve their ability to think and behave rationally while, in fact, stimulants impair this ability. Students under the effects of stimulants lose their ability to interpret conflicts objectively and thus might start fights and become violent. Students need to understand the importance of keeping a clear head to discuss disagreements in a logical and rational fashion and to behave rationally when dealing with others.

2. **Introduction:** The teacher will ask the following questions:

   ◗ **Do alcohol and other stimulants affect your thinking, judgment and actions?**

   ◗ **How does one notice the change in a person?**

   ◗ **Do reactions slow down?**

   ◗ **What happens to your walking, driving, speech, etc.?**

   The teacher will point out that since the use of stimulants decreases the person's reaction time and the person's ability to coordinate movements, it is most important to refrain from taking stimulants prior to operating any machinery, equipment, etc. The inability to function properly could cause injury and even death.

   The teacher relates the following story:

   > **John and Mary were at a party at Bill's house. Bill's parents were out of town. Someone had brought a keg of beer to the party. During the evening Mary noticed that John had quite a few beers. (Mary had only soft drinks.) When it was time to go, John started to brag in a loud voice how fast his car could go and how much fun it would be to drive home in a fast car. Mary was concerned because she knew that high speed can cause accidents and injury especially when alcohol clouds clear thinking; also, if stopped by the police, John could be in big trouble with the law, lose his license and would really disappoint his parents. What do you think Mary should do?**

   The teacher can then discuss the importance of having a clear head by avoiding the use of stimulants.

3. **Identify the Skill Components:** Write the following skill components on the board or on sentence strips:

1. Assess the situation.
2. Identify irrational behaviors.
3. Identify the reasons for such behavior.
4. Decide to take control.
5. Think of a rational solution.
6. Consider safety first.
7. Exercise your plan.

4. *Model the Skill:* The teacher can model an incident where two former friends, Mary and Henry, are at the same picnic. The teacher will have a student portray one of the former friends who has had too much beer and is feeling bold and aggressive. This person tries to get back at his/her former friend for stealing his/her girlfriend/boyfriend. The teacher will role play the other former friend who is sober and will show by the use of the skill components how rational thinking can resolve the situation.

5. *Behavioral Rehearsal:*

   A. *Selection:* The teacher will select two pairs of students to role play.

   B. *Role Play:* One pair of students will role play the story in the introduction. The other pair of students will role play the scene described in the "Model the Skill" section.

   C. *Completion:* The teacher and the students in the audience will analyze the role play and the use of the skill components. If corrections are necessary, the role playing students will be asked by the teacher to re-enact the role play. If no corrections are needed, the role play is complete.

   D. *Reinforcers:* The teacher will thank the students who participated in the role plays for their well done role plays and praise them highly for any special performance.

   E. *Discussion:* The teacher will encourage discussion from the class regarding any personal experiences which students would like to share. The teacher can review the points made in the introduction where rational behavior and clear thinking were discussed.

6. *Practice:* The teacher will ask the students to complete the worksheet "A Clear Head" in class and to discuss it after completion.

7. *Independent Use:* The teacher will ask the students to go to the library to find an article on rational thinking. After reading the article, students will write a one-page report on how rational thinking can help prevent violent behavior and violent situations. Students will return the report in one week and will share their reports in class.

8. *Continuation:* The teacher will indicate that there are many occasions in adult life where it is most important to have a clear head and that, therefore, stimulants should never be used to any extent since they will cloud the judgment and decision-making process. The teacher will refer to this lesson frequently during the school year and always emphasize that the use of stimulants by adults is often the consequence of having started the bad habit at a young age and that the students should abstain from using stimulants in order to safeguard their future.

Name _____ Date _____

A CLEAR HEAD

Directions: Complete the worksheet by filling in the blanks with an appropriate word selected from the box below. Then describe an example or a situation to illustrate each of the statements.

For someone who is under the influence of stimulants:

1. Thinking is _____.

   Example/Situation: _____

   _____

2. Reasoning is _____.

   Example/Situation: _____

   _____

3. Memory is _____.

   Example/Situation: _____

   _____

For someone who has had no stimulants:

1. Judgment is _____.

   Example/Situation: _____

   _____

2. Memory is _____.

   Example/Situation: _____

   _____

A Clear Head *(cont'd)*

3. Thinking is _____.

    Example/Situation: _____

    _____

inaccurate	clear
impaired	rational
faulty	precise

Controlling Depressive Feelings

Behavioral Objective: Students will learn that stimulants, including cigarettes and alcohol, can affect emotions in powerful and uncontrollable ways (excessive anger, jealousy, paranoia, carelessness and risktaking) and that they must and can control their depressive feelings and emotions without resorting to drugs.

Directed Lessons:

1. **Establish the Need:** Youth often believe that stimulants, including cigarettes and alcohol, can help them control and improve depressive feelings. Even though some stimulants can diminish feelings such as sadness and anger for a short time, they will, in the end, distort reality and lead to inappropriate emotional reactions and promote misinterpretation of communication. Students should be made aware that it is illegal to buy, distribute, and consume certain stimulants (alcohol up to age 21, cigarettes up to age 18, all others for youngsters and adults). Students must learn that they can control their feelings and emotions without the use of stimulants.

2. **Introduction:** The teacher will ask the students to name feelings and emotions which they think could be controlled, improved, and minimized by the use of stimulants and will ask a student to list them on the board. They might include:

    sadness, happiness, depression, sexual appeal, popularity, etc.

    The teacher will then discuss with the students the effects stimulants can have on the feelings and emotions listed on the board and point out that the students' beliefs, namely that benefits are derived from the use of stimulants, is a myth, which is spread in advertisements for reasons of sale and greed. The teacher will emphasize that the real effects of stimulant use lead to non-beneficial consequences such as low self-esteem, withdrawal from others, no close friendships, and depression.

    The teacher can then emphasize that according to statistics cigarettes and alcohol can be addictive, and that students who use those stimulants are more easily tempted to progress to more addictive hard core drugs such as cocaine and heroin.

3. **Identify the Skill Components:** Write the following skill components on the board or on sentence strips:

    1. Analyze the reasons that cause depressive feelings.
    2. If you desire stimulants, ask yourself why.
    3. Identify the depressive feelings that make you want to use stimulants.
    4. Realize the harm stimulants can do.

5. Identify the consequences of stimulant use.

6. Select appropriate and more satisfying activities to control and subdue these feelings.

7. Make the right decision.

4. ***Model the Skill:*** The teacher will ask one student to play the part of a person who has just lost his/her best friend in a car accident. This person feels so bad that he/she can think of nothing else but to try stimulants to make him/her feel better. The teacher will try to make the student see that stimulants will not help and that there are other ways to get relief. The teacher will use the skill components to help the student realize how to control his/her emotion.

5. ***Behavioral Rehearsal:***

    A. *Selection:* The teacher will divide the class into 5 or 6 groups.

    B. *Role Play:* The teacher will ask each group to brainstorm events or situations which might have created depressive feelings. Each group will role play such a situation to show how they can use the skill components to control such feelings.

    C. *Completion:* After each role play, the teacher will reinforce correct behaviors, identify inappropriate behaviors and ask the students to re-enact the role play with corrections, if necessary. If there are no corrections, role play is complete.

    D. *Reinforcers:* The teacher will thank the groups for their participation in performing the role plays, and give special praise to the best group's role play.

    E. *Discussion:* The teacher will encourage discussion of how feelings and emotions can be controlled and how stimulants can increase depression and make it impossible to control feelings and emotions.

6. ***Practice:*** The teacher will distribute the worksheet "Control" for students to complete and discuss in class.

7. ***Independent Use:*** The teacher will hand out copies of the worksheet "Control Interviews" for students to complete at home and return to class in one week for discussion with the entire class.

8. ***Continuation:*** The teacher will stress at all times that stimulants do not improve feelings or increase self-esteem. As situations occur, he/she will emphasize that feelings and emotions can be effectively controlled by performing appropriate activities. He/she will suggest the use of the skill components to help students control their feelings and emotions by other means than taking stimulants.

Name _____ Date _____

CONTROL

Directions: Complete the following sentences using specific situations.

1. I feel sad at school when _____

    _____

2. I feel angry at home when _____

    _____

3. I feel frustrated with my friends when _____

    _____

Directions: Complete the following sentences using specific items to control very depressive feelings and emotions. Employ the skill components to determine what to do.

When I feel very sad I _____

_____

When I feel extremely angry I _____

_____

When I feel most frustrated I _____

_____

When I feel depressed I _____

_____

Why would you do those things, and how would doing so help to subdue these feelings?

_____

_____

_____

_____

_____

_____

Name _____ Date _____

CONTROL INTERVIEWS

Directions: Interview two adults from your family or adult friends and record how they have learned to control overwhelming feelings of the emotions indicated in each box.

ANGER	SADNESS
1.	1.
2.	2.
DEPRESSION	FRUSTRATION
1.	1.
2.	2.

Indicate who the person is (mother, father, uncle, neighbor, etc.), not their name.

Person #1 is _____.

Person #2 is _____.

Counteracting the Desire for Using Stimulants

Behavioral Objective: Students will learn how to select pleasant and absorbing activities to counteract their desire for using stimulants, so that they can resist stimulant use even under strong peer pressure and high stress. They will also learn to use their knowledge about the effects of stimulants on behavior, health and attitude to assist peers who are addicted to desist taking stimulants.

Directed Lesson:

1. **Establish the Need:** Teenagers have a strong desire to use stimulants in order to, what they believe, make them feel "high" and socially more acceptable. Sometimes they will use them only out of curiosity to find out how it feels. Other times they will reach for stimulants especially when urged on by peers since they are convinced that taking stimulants is the only means to improve their feelings when problems arise, such as loneliness, depression, grade failure, losing a girl/boyfriend, etc. They have to learn that this is a myth, that, in fact, stimulants increase depression, and that there are other activities available which should be employed to dampen or temporarily forget those problems. These activities will improve their feelings to a much greater degree than stimulants and without negative consequences of illegality, depression, violence, crime and even suicide. The students will learn the benefits they can derive from other pleasant and absorbing activities and how to select them.

2. **Introduction:** The teacher will state that the purchase, sale, and use of stimulants and other drugs to students is illegal and stimulants' reactions can produce unsafe behaviors, unstable emotions and health problems. (The teacher may want to review the behaviors, emotions and health problems.)

   The teacher will ask the following questions:

   - **Who can be tempted to take stimulants?**
   - **Why do you feel you might want to take stimulants?**
   - **Is it because your peers do so and want you to join them?**
   - **Are you wanting to do it to forget your problems?**
   - **Will it solve your problems?**
   - **What can be the consequences for taking stimulants?**
   - **How can other activities counteract your desire for taking stimulants?**

   The teacher will then ask the students to name some activities that might help them to counteract their desire for taking stimulants, be it because of peer pressure, curiosity or to forget their unhappy feelings due to problems. The teacher will ask one student to list these activities on the board when the other students call them out, such as:

Sports—individual, team

Music—dance, chorus, band, orchestra

Debate team

Student government

Yearbook

Dramatics

School newspaper

Games, cards, board games

3. ***Identify the Skill Components:*** Write the following skill components on the board or on sentence strips:

1. Analyze the reasons for the desire to take stimulants.

2. Analyze the feelings that led to the desire.

3. Think of the immediate consequences.

4. Think of the long-term consequences.

5. Define other activities to dampen the unwanted feelings.

6. Choose an activity.

7. Try other activities.

8. Realize that anything is better than becoming addicted.

9. Be assured of final success.

4. ***Model the Skill:*** The teacher relates her/his own experience with a very happy teen, the same age as the class, who failed in math and became terribly depressed. He was an easy convert for taking stimulants; therefore, the teacher kept an eye on him. Indeed very soon the teacher observed that this teen was pressured by a group of peers to join them in trying out some new type of inhalant they had discovered which they claimed was excellent against depression since it lifted unhappy feelings to very "high." The teacher called the teen in for a talk to dissuade him from succumbing to the peers. The teacher succeeded by using the skill component to guide him/her during the conversation. The teen chose to join a running team and soon excelled. His self-esteem improved because of his success as a runner, which helped him to improve his performance in math. Thus, the teen was happy again. The teen is played by one of the teacher's students and should select any activity he/she prefers.

5. ***Behavioral Rehearsal:***

A. *Selection:* The teacher will select two students to role play. Other pairs of students will be selected, as time permits, to do similar role plays.

B. *Role Play:* The first two students will role play Joe and Bob "hanging out" on a Saturday afternoon. Joe tries to get Bob to get "high" by inhaling the fumes from a lighter. Bob resists this coercion using the skill components. He even persuades Joe to stop taking inhalants and instead to engage in a safe and healthy activity.

Other role plays can be suggested and enacted by the students, based on their own experience or those of friends, as time permits.

C. *Completion:* The teacher and class will determine if the role play was done correctly and if the skill components were used in the role play. If not, the teacher will ask the students to re-enact the role play with corrections; if yes, the role play is complete.

D. *Reinforcers:* The teacher will compliment the role players for their performance and participation and their good work.

E. *Discussion:* The teacher will engage the class in a discussion about the difficulties they may have to resist stimulants under strong peer pressure. The teacher might ask the students whether discussing this now and learning about the adverse effects of stimulants and the use of the skill components could help them to resist stimulants if they find themselves being subjected to such peer pressure. The teacher should also discuss the healthy beneficial activities the students might want to join.

6. **Practice:** The teacher will divide the class into four or five groups. Each group will be given a large piece of paper and markers. The teacher will ask each group of students to develop lists on the following topics:

1. Reasons and excuses for using stimulants.

2. Consequences incurred when using stimulants.

3. Safe/healthy activities to do instead of using stimulants.

The students will brainstorm and list as many items as possible. After 10 minutes' time, each group will share its list with the whole class.

7. **Independent Use:** The teacher will ask the students to complete, at home, the worksheet "Healthy Activities" and discuss the completed worksheet with their parents. The teacher will ask that the students return the completed worksheet to class in one week and share their own and their parents' comments and reactions.

8. **Continuation:** The teacher will point out the consequences of stimulant use, which can include violent situations, health problems and legal complications. The teacher will especially emphasize the use of other activities that have no serious consequences to counteract their desires for stimulants. He/she will point out that excelling in those activities might have additional benefits, as was demonstrated in the actual story used by the teacher when modeling the skill.

Name _____ Date _____

HEALTHY ACTIVITIES

Follow the instructions below to complete this exercise. Share it with your parents and ask for their input.

Directions: List three safe/healthy activities to do instead of using stimulants and explain why these activities would be effective for you.

ACTIVITY #1 _____

_____

_____

ACTIVITY #2 _____

_____

_____

ACTIVITY #3 _____

_____

_____

What would you tell a group of peers when they try to sell you stimulants and to ask you to join them in a stimulant party? Explain your answer in a paragraph.

Understanding That Marijuana Is a Dangerous Stimulant

Behavioral Objective: Students will learn to understand that marijuana has the same effects on body and mind as other stimulants and its use will lead to addiction.

Directed Lesson:

1. **Establish the Need:** Young people frequently believe that marijuana is a "safe" stimulant which they can use for experimentation with no serious consequences. Students have to learn that this is not correct and have to realize that marijuana is an illegal drug and that using it is against the law. They also need to be aware of the detrimental effect marijuana has on mind, body and spirit and that it can become a habit and create yearning for harder drugs.

2. **Introduction:** The teacher will read this story to the class:

   Robert was an above average student who sometimes made the honor roll. One day he went to visit his cousin. When he arrived at his cousin's house, he found him with three other friends. After spending some time trying to decide where to go, his cousin said that he had some marijuana and that before they went anywhere, they should smoke a few joints. Robert kept saying that he was not interested in smoking marijuana, but he kept getting pressured by his own cousin and his friends who kept reassuring him that nothing would happen and that he would enjoy the "high." Robert gave in and joined the others in smoking the marijuana. He found that he enjoyed it and liked the feeling of being high as he found himself laughing and giggling at everything. Robert liked his experience so much that he asked where he could buy some for himself.

   The teacher will ask the class:

   ▶ **Why did Robert go from saying no to smoking marijuana, to using it, and eventually buying it for himself?**

   ▶ **What will happen to him if he continues to use marijuana?**

3. **Identify the Skill Components:** Write the following skill components on the board or on transparencies to be used with an overhead projector, or on sentence strips:

   1. Evaluate the situation.
   2. Identify the problem.
   3. Identify if peer pressure has been applied.
   4. Re-identify the effects stimulant use can cause.
   5. Realize that marijuana is a stimulant.

6. Consider the possible consequences of using marijuana.

7. Decide what you should do in this situation.

8. Act accordingly.

9. Live according to your choice.

4. ***Model the Skill:*** The teacher pretends to be a student who is being pressured by three friends to smoke marijuana with them. He/she will use the skill components to deal with the peer pressure.

5. ***Behavioral Rehearsal:***

   A. *Selection:* The teacher will choose four groups of students for role playing. (The number of groups will depend on the time available for the exercise.)

   B. *Role Play:* The teacher will ask each group of students to role play using one of the four following situations. The rest of the class will watch the role plays and how the skill components are applied by the actors. The four role play situations are:

      – A younger student starts associating with older students who have been smoking marijuana for a long time; thus they are exhibiting signs of stimulant abuse.

      – A student sees his brother/sister smoking a joint.

      – A student sees a parent smoking marijuana.

      – A student becomes encouraged to try marijuana after hearing and reading about it.

   C. *Completion:* After each role play the teacher will reinforce correct behaviors, identify inappropriate behaviors and ask students to re-enact role play with corrections. If there are no corrections, role play is complete.

   D. *Reinforcers:* The teacher will give verbal and non-verbal praise (specific) for correct behavior.

   E. *Discussion:* Upon the conclusion of each role play, the teacher will ask the students to relate how they would react in a similar situation, how the skill components could help them stay drug free and what problems they might encounter.

6. ***Practice:*** The teacher will distribute copies of the following word search, "Synonyms" and ask the students to find the words that are associated with marijuana in the puzzle. When they have finished, the teacher will ask them to write a short story using some of the words found in the word search on the back of the puzzle page. After completing their short story, the teacher will ask them to write out the skill components as they relate to their story.

7. ***Independent Use:*** The teacher will give students copies of the worksheet "Effects of Marijuana" to complete outside of class after they have done some research. They are to list some of the short-term and long-term effects of marijuana and to report back to the class verbally, and in writing, the results of their efforts in one week. The class will then compose a master list and post it in the room.

8. ***Continuation:*** The teacher will remind the class that marijuana causes numerous short-term and long-term effects to the user's body and mind and that marijuana use could lead to heavier drug use of more potent and dangerous substances. The students should be encouraged to resist the temptation to "just try it once."

Name _____ Date _____

SYNONYMS

Directions: The following words that are associated with marijuana are found in the puzzle below. They may be horizontal, vertical, or diagonal, and they may be spelled forwards or backwards. (Number 21 is on two lines.) Find each of the words and circle them.

1. Acapulco Gold
2. Bhang
3. Blunt
4. Cannabis
5. Drug
6. Effects
7. Ganja

8. Grass
9. Hay
10. Jive
11. Joint
12. Laughing Grass
13. Loo Weed
14. Mary Jane

15. Pot
16. Reefer
17. Rope
18. Sinsemilla
19. Tea
20. Texas Tea
21. Thai Sticks
22. Weed

A	B	C	D	E	F	C	T	H	A	I	S	G	H	I
J	M	A	R	Y	J	A	N	E	S	T	I	C	K	S
K	L	M	U	N	O	N	P	Q	G	G	N	A	H	B
L	A	U	G	H	I	N	G	G	R	A	S	S	R	S
O	T	U	V	W	G	A	N	J	A	X	E	Y	J	Z
O	Z	X	W	N	L	B	M	A	S	F	M	P	O	T
W	E	E	D	B	J	I	V	E	S	C	I	D	I	E
E	F	F	E	C	T	S	F	R	G	B	L	U	N	T
E	A	C	A	P	U	L	C	O	G	O	L	D	T	H
D	I	R	E	E	F	E	R	P	J	H	A	Y	K	L
M	N	T	E	A	O	P	T	E	X	A	S	T	E	A

SYNONYMS

Answer Key

A	B	C	D	E	F	C	T	H	A	I	S	G	H	I
J	M	A	R	Y	J	A	N	E	S	T	I	C	K	S
K	L	M	U	N	O	N	P	Q	G	G	N	A	H	B
L	A	U	G	H	I	N	G	G	R	A	S	S	R	S
O	T	U	V	W	G	A	N	J	A	X	E	Y	J	Z
O	Z	X	W	N	L	B	M	A	S	F	M	P	O	T
W	E	E	D	B	J	I	V	E	S	C	I	D	I	E
E	F	F	E	C	T	S	F	R	G	B	L	U	N	T
E	A	C	A	P	U	L	C	O	G	O	L	D	T	H
D	I	R	E	E	F	E	R	P	J	H	A	Y	K	L
M	N	T	E	A	O	P	T	E	X	A	S	T	E	A

Name _____ Date _____

EFFECTS OF MARIJUANA

I. Please list the *short-term* effects of marijuana use.

    1. _____

    2. _____

    3. _____

    4. _____

    5. _____

    6. _____

    7. _____

II. Please list the *long-term* effects of marijuana use.

    1. _____

    2. _____

    3. _____

    4. _____

    5. _____

    6. _____

    7. _____

Understanding the Effects of Using Household Products as Inhalants

Behavioral Objective: Students will know not to be tempted to use easy-to-get household products as inhalants since they will learn to understand the serious consequences these inhalants can inflict on body and mind which, in fact, can lead to longtime sickness and even death.

Directed Lessons:

1. **Establish the Need:** One of the fastest growing areas of chemical abuse is the use of inhalants, which can cause serious sickness and even death. These inhalants have become the chemical of choice by youth mainly because they are inexpensive and can be purchased at most stores. There are hundreds of easily available household products that can be used to get high. Understanding inhalants and their effects will help students in making wise decisions about activities affecting their lives.

2. **Introduction:** Read this story to the class:

   Michael was an average student who tended to be more of a follower than a leader. If he was in a class and did an activity with other boys who were wearing their pants below their hips, he also would do the same thing.

   While on his way to school one day, Michael met up with a group of his friends. Because of the way that they were acting, he knew something was up. Pretty soon, one of his friends asked him if he wanted a "quick" high. They told Michael to hold a paper bag over his nose and to take some deep breaths. After a few times of taking deep breaths from the bag, Michael started to lose touch with his surroundings. He felt "high" and wanted to know what he was breathing in from the paper bag. His friends told him that they had sprayed drops of butane starter fluid in the bag.

   For the next few days, Michael would meet with this same group of friends. Each day they had something different that they used to get high. One day it was smelling fumes from metallic paint, other days it was air freshener, then rubber cement, and even white-out correctional fluid.

   On Friday, the group decided to spray breath freshener straight up their noses in addition to breathing in the butane from unlit cigarette lighters up each nostril. This time Michael experienced great difficulty in trying to walk. He also kept losing his balance. When he entered the school, he was experiencing extreme headaches.

161

At lunch time, Michael did not have any appetite but remained in the cafeteria. After a few minutes, he started to experience a loss of self-control and began to vomit. He eventually passed out and had to be rushed to the nearest local hospital.

At the hospital, Michael learned how close he had come to suffocating and dying. The doctor told him that the unfiltered chemicals that he inhaled were going straight to his brain and were beginning to affect his body. He also told Michael about the increase in hospital visits by people suffering from the use of inhalants, and that there exist about 1,000 household products that can be used as inhalants.

Michael realized how close he came to dying and vowed to never again use inhalants and to be around anyone who does.

The teacher will ask the class: "How do you think Michael got so involved with inhalants that they almost cost him his life?"

3. ***Identify the Skill Components:*** Write the following skill components on the board or on transparencies to be used with an overhead projector, or on sentence strips:

1. Evaluate the reason for participating in an activity.

2. Analyze the consequences.

3. Weigh the harm against the pleasure.

4. Think of the longtime consequences.

5. Consider your lifetime goals.

6. Consider another activity for divergence.

7. Decide if you need outside help.

8. Decide whom to ask for help.

9. Make a wise choice.

4. ***Model the Skill:*** The teacher will role play Michael from the story in the introduction after Michael realizes the consequences to his health from the use of inhalants. The teacher, being Michael, will use the skill components to show how they can help in the thought process and decision making so that Michael will not succumb to the pressure of peers to join a stimulant-inhaling party.

5. ***Behavioral Rehearsal:***

A. *Selection:* The teacher will select three pairs of students for enacting role plays.

B. *Role Play:* Each pair of students will role play one of the following scenarios using the skill components:

- Jim is being pressured by his girlfriend to "get high" with her by using aerosol as an inhalant.

- Nikki, age 16, comes home from school and finds her younger brother and his friend sniffing inhalants from a paper bag.

– While cleaning the garage, Don and Mary, who are siblings, find several items that they know can be used to get high if they inhale them. They are wondering and discussing how it would feel and are very much tempted to try one.

C. *Completion:* After each role play, the teacher will reinforce correct behaviors, identify inappropriate behaviors and ask the students to re-enact the role play with corrections. If there are no corrections, role play is complete.

D. *Reinforcers:* The teacher will give verbal and nonverbal praise (specific) for correct behavior.

E. *Discussion:* The teacher leads the discussion by asking the following questions:

▶ **Why is getting "high" so tempting?**

▶ **What can be the consequences when using household inhalants or any other stimulants?**

▶ **Is it legal to use household inhalants as stimulants?**

▶ **How sick can you get from inhaling household stimulants?**

▶ **What activity could you pursue in order to forget the temptation to indulge in the use of inhalants to get high?**

6. ***Practice:*** The teacher will distribute copies of the worksheet "Household Products" for students to complete and discuss in class.

7. ***Independent Use:*** The teacher will give the students copies of the worksheet "Consequences" to take home and return completed in one week for discussion in class.

8. ***Continuation:*** The teacher will emphasize the importance of avoiding the use of household inhalants by reiterating the serious consequences the use of these stimulants can have on body and brain and future goals.

Name _____ Date _____

HOUSEHOLD PRODUCTS

Directions: List the most common house-hold products that can be used to inhale as stimulants for getting high and list the consequences to your body and mind caused by their use. Then list activities that could help you to avoid using stimulants and the consequences these activities present.

Stimulants: **Consequences:**

Activities: **Consequences:**

Tell in a one-paragraph story how you managed to avoid participating in a stimulant party when pressured by your schoolmates to join. (Use the skill components.)

Name _____ Date _____

CONSEQUENCES

Directions: Do research in the library and/or on the Internet to identify some of the serious health problems that can result from inhaling household products. Report in one or two pages what you found out and how using inhalants could affect the user's immediate and future achievements and goals.

Understanding the Danger from Using "Gateway" Drugs

Behavioral Objective: Students will learn to understand that even soft "gateway" stimulants, such as tobacco and beer, are addictive and certainly harmful and can lead to the use of hard drugs and to worse addiction. Therefore, students will become sensible and refrain from the temptation of starting to consume, smoke, and inhale even those soft stimulants.

Directed Lessons:

1. **Establish the Need:** Adolescents frequently believe that the soft stimulants, also called "gateway" drugs, like tobacco, beer, and household chemicals are safe to use for getting "high". These stimulants are called "gateway" drugs since they are known to open the gate to the consumption of hard drugs because they are not safe but addictive and harmful. Therefore, students will have to realize that by starting to consume those stimulants they might prepare themselves to become hard-drug users. Tobacco, one of the "gateway" drugs, has now been identified by the Attorney General to be not only harmful but also addictive. Other researchers have shown that a significant proportion of marijuana smokers and hard drug users began to smoke tobacco cigarettes at an early age. Youth need to understand that the cycle of drug use starts with soft "gateway" drugs and leads to the consumption of hard and harder drugs and that therefore it is best for them to abstain from any use of stimulants.

2. **Introduction:** The teacher will mention that the warning that appears on tobacco products unfortunately is not specific enough as the students will see when they receive the practice sheet that will be distributed at the end of class. Then the teacher will read the following scenario to the class:

   Jay was a bright young man of 15 who had an excellent grade-point average. He was taking the regular ninth grade classes as all of you do. Because of his above average ability, he was taking a foreign language, advanced math (geometry), and participated in the band. He also attended many of the school's sporting events immediately after school and on weekends. In spite of his parents' dislike and warning, he often "snuck" a cigarette. He had "good" friends who also had other "good" friends.

   Late one evening, after a game, he and his three buddies, Ralph, Ramon, and Willie, went to another friend's home. There they watched a video, drank coke, and ate chips. Two of the "friends" were heavy smokers and could not resist—so they lit up. Jay had not taken his cigarettes with him and was offered supplies to wrap one. He carefully rolled the tobacco into the paper and enjoyed his smoke. Throughout the evening, others smoked their "products" and described their

feelings about the "smoke," briefly. One of Ramon's "friends" told Jay of the special quality of his smoke, offering one to Jay.

After Jay's "experiment" with this new product—a rolled cigarette—he thought that he was feeling much better.

In the course of the evening, Jay made arrangements to meet Ramon again, perhaps during school hours, for a visit and smoke. Subsequent to that, they became closer acquaintances. Within months, Jay had quit the band and was dropped from language and geometry classes because of his poor grades.

3. ***Identify the Skill Components:*** Write the following skill components on the board or on sentence strips:

   1. Consider the danger of "gateway" stimulants.
   2. Consider the potential consequences when using these stimulants.
   3. Analyze your previous and present accomplishments.
   4. Keep in mind your life's goals.
   5. Weigh the disadvantages against feeling "good."
   6. Consider the possibility of addiction, etc.
   7. Make a wise and healthy choice.

4. ***Model the Skill:*** The teacher will use the scenario in the introduction to model the skill. He or she will model the skill by describing his/her "thinking process" beyond the initial introduction of Jay to Ramon, using the skill components and giving particular emphasis to:

   – leaving school to join Ramon in a smoke;
   – sharing the rolled cigarette (joint);
   – smoking something "heavier" as offered by Ramon;
   – the decrease in Jay's accomplishments, his life's goals, etc.

5. ***Behavioral Rehearsal:***

   A. *Selection:* The teacher will select two groups of five students to re-enact a scenario similar to that described in the introduction.

   B. *Role Play:* Both groups of five will role play a similar scenario to that in the introduction and Jay will use the skill components to make a choice about what is best for him to do.

   C. *Completion:* After each role play, the teacher will highlight correct responses, correct errors, and have students redo the role play, as necessary. If there are no corrections, the role play is completed.

   D. *Reinforcers:* The teacher and peers will thank the students for doing the role plays well and for appropriately completing the role plays using the skill components. The class will identify the better of the two role plays and provide special recognition to participants for their efforts.

E. *Discussion:* The class, with the teacher's leadership, will discuss the role plays and identify other potential consequences due to the use of stimulants than those portrayed in the role plays.

6. Practice: The teacher will distribute and ask the students to complete the worksheet "Warning" and select students other than those who participated in the role play to discuss their responses with the class.

7. Independent Use: The teacher will ask the students to interview an adult or a much older friend and complete the "Tunnel to the Future" worksheet for homework. It should be returned within one week for discussion in class.

8. Continuation: The teacher will review consequences from the use of "hazardous" stimulants periodically and share related current news releases with the class throughout the year.

WARNING

Why Should We Avoid Indulging in This Product?

Directions: Select a Stimulant and describe how the use of it could affect you and others, such as family numbers, relatives, co-workers, and friends, in regard to the five environmental items listed in the table.

THE SELECTED STIMULANT IS:

Item	You	Others You Know:
Home		
School		
Career		
Health		
Relationships		

Considering the skill components, make a statement (one paragraph) which reflects your "considered" opinion of what to do. Use the back of this page, if needed.

_____   _____
Name   Date

TUNNEL TO THE FUTURE

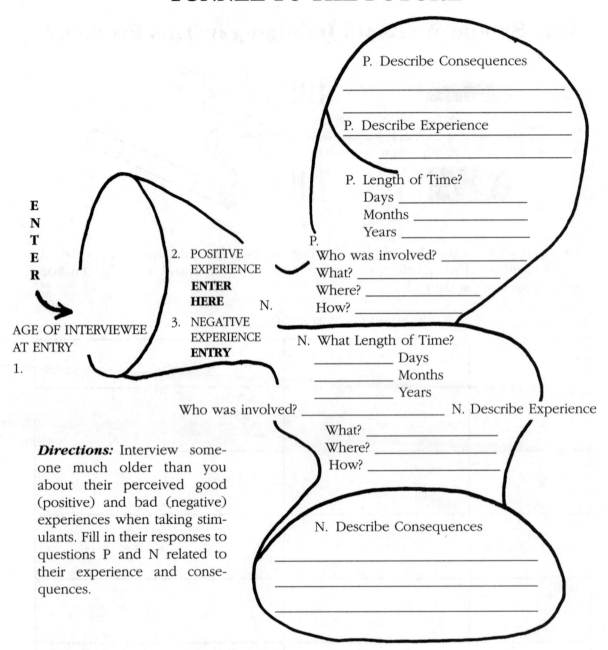

P. Describe Consequences

_____

_____

P. Describe Experience _____

_____

P. Length of Time?
Days _____
Months _____
Years _____

P.

Who was involved? _____
What? _____
Where? _____
How? _____

E N T E R

AGE OF INTERVIEWEE
AT ENTRY

1.

2. POSITIVE
EXPERIENCE
**ENTER
HERE**

3. NEGATIVE
EXPERIENCE
ENTRY

N.

N. What Length of Time?
_____ Days
_____ Months
_____ Years

Who was involved? _____   N. Describe Experience

What? _____
Where? _____
How? _____

Directions: Interview someone much older than you
about their perceived good
(positive) and bad (negative)
experiences when taking stimulants. Fill in their responses to
questions P and N related to
their experience and consequences.

N. Describe Consequences

_____

_____

_____

© 1998 by John Wiley & Sons, Inc.

QUESTIONS TO ASK INTERVIEWEE

1. How old were you when you first used the stimulant?
2. Describe the experience fully (i.e., who was involved, what was the stimulant, how was it used).
3. What length of time elapsed before you noticed the consequences?
4. What were the results to self, health, career, safety, etc.?

_____   _____
Name   Date

Reacting to Behavior Indicative of Stimulant and Drug Abuse

Behavioral Objective: Students will learn how to recognize the symptoms of stimulant and drug abuse and how to act accordingly. This knowledge is important for the students to have so that they will realize the serious consequences in behavioral change and thus better understand the reasons for subduing any desires for stimulant and drug use, even under the heading "experimental." This knowledge will also make it possible to recognize peers who have become stimulant addicts and empower them to seek professional assistance.

Directed Lesson:

1. **Establish the Need:** Students are often concerned about the behavior of some of their peers. In some instances they would like to help them and include them in their group activities. To do so, students have to learn to understand and recognize the reasons why some of their peers seem to change their behavior and become difficult to deal with and impossibly negative when asked to participate in group activities. One reason for their strange behavior might be that these students have become addicted to using one or another stimulant to get a feeling of "high" and do not realize themselves how their social behavior has changed. The symptoms of stimulant abuse, such as chemical substance abuse, are not always clearly recognizable but there are certain symptoms that occur most frequently. Learning these symptoms will teach the students to empower addicted peers to seek professional assistance and, more important, will make the students realize the serious consequences, namely negative change in social behavior and attitude, that stimulants can cause and therefore make it easier for the students to subdue any desires to experiment with stimulants or any other drug.

2. **Introduction:** The teacher will tell the following story to the class:

   Mr. Mack was the kind of teacher who truly loved and cared for all of his students. Whenever students had problems they could discuss them with this teacher, and he would do what he could to help them with a solution.

   It was just after the students had returned from their spring vacation that Mr. Mack started to notice a real change in the behavior of four students. One of the first things he saw was a change in each student's personality.

   There was a general change in their mood. They seemed depressed and had a negative and critical outlook on everything. The students started withdrawing from interactions with other students. The only time they seemed to interact was when they were trying to borrow money from the other students. When a student wouldn't loan them any money, they became verbally and physically abusive. It was also during this time that Mr. Mack started getting reports of things being stolen from students, such as clothing, money, Walkmans™ and CD players.

When the teacher questioned the students about their knowledge of items that were stolen, the four became very defensive and increasingly angry and defiant. They each had elaborate stories or excuses that resulted in frequent lies. They exhibited an inability to reason or think logically, had memory loss, and feelings of paranoia.

As days passed, the teacher noticed overall changes in their physical appearance. Each of the four began to appear run down and started exhibiting other physical symptoms, such as slurred speech, loss of coordination, loss of memory, trembling, and a dreamy or blank expression.

There also was a decline in the personal hygiene of these students. They began to appear unkempt and wore the same clothes day after day. Their complexions began to appear unhealthy. They looked pale or flushed. Their eyes also looked bloodshot and their pupils were dilated or constricted.

Each of the four students demonstrated a decline in their school performance also. Their grades fell and they did no school homework. They showed no interest in extracurricular activities; in fact, they dropped out of athletics and other clubs. Their behavior became more and more problematic as they continually got in trouble for cutting classes, truancy, fighting, theft, and other unacceptable conduct.

One day while the class was in session, the principal and members of the local police department appeared at Mr. Mack's classroom because of a complaint made by another student's parent. The parent said that the four students tried to sell drugs to his son. Consequently, the students and their lockers were searched by the police. Since drugs and drug paraphernalia were found, the students were arrested. Each of the four students was then expelled from the school.

The teacher asks the class: What are the symptoms of stimulant abuse that were exhibited by the four students? The teacher and students will discuss and identify as many symptoms as possible and list them on the board.

3. *Identify the Skill Components:* Write the following skill components on the board or on transparencies to be used with an overhead projector, or on sentence strips.

   1. Observe the person(s) closely.

   2. Evaluate the behavior.

   3. Evaluate the attitude.

   4. Identify the problem.

   5. Re-identify the symptoms of stimulant and other drug abuse.

   6. Decide if the symptoms are due to stimulant or drug addiction.

   7. Analyze the consequences of continued abuse.

8. Decide what to do in the situation.

9. Make a decision to act.

10. Follow through with your decision.

4. *Model the Skill:* The teacher will demonstrate the skill by using the skill components to show how to assist one of his/her students in a situation in which the student suspects a friend to be addicted to using a chemical substance, since he/she shows the symptoms of being addicted to stimulants.

5. *Behavioral Rehearsal:*

A. *Selection:* The teacher will choose several groups of four students for role playing. (The number of groups will depend on the time available for the exercise.)

B. *Role Play:* The teacher will ask two students to enact symptoms that are typical for persons to show when they are addicted to stimulants. (Some of the symptoms to be used are listed below.) The other two students will role play how they feel about these peers who show symptoms of stimulant abuse and how they can assist them. They will also role play their reaction to stimulant abuse in general.

   – Students exhibit various physical problems (unsteady walk, slurred speech, etc.) that are symptoms of stimulant abuse.

   – Teacher has a discussion with a couple of students about their decline in school performance that may be symptoms of stimulant abuse.

   – Students act out various personality and emotional changes that may be symptoms of stimulant abuse.

   – Student goes through a number of situations that are causing a disruption of family relations that may be symptoms of stimulant abuse.

   – Students show various drug-specific indicators that may be symptoms of stimulant abuse.

C. *Completion:* After each role play, the teacher will reinforce correct behavior, identify inappropriate behaviors, and re-enact role play with corrections. If there are no corrections, role play is complete.

D. *Reinforcers:* The teacher will give verbal and non-verbal praise (specific) for correct behavior.

E. *Discussion:* Upon the conclusion of each role play the students may relate how they would react in a similar situation. Students should discuss any difficulties they may have encountered while trying to help a friend deal with the chemical substance abuse or another stimulant abuse.

6. *Practice:* The teacher will distribute copies of the worksheet "Reactions" for students to complete and discuss in class.

7. *Independent Use:* The teacher will ask the students to select one of the following topics to research for a two-page typewritten paper:

- Signs of Drug Abuse
- Signs of Physical Deterioration
- Dramatic Changes in School Performance
- Changes in Behavior

The students will report back to the class in one week. They will relate verbally the steps they used to do the research and discuss their two-page report and hand it in.

8. ***Continuation:*** The teacher will point out that changing patterns of performance, appearance, and behavior may indicate symptoms of stimulant or other drug abuse. By being able to identify these symptoms, they may be in a position to assist individuals in seeking appropriate help and by realizing how detestable these changes caused by stimulant abuse are, they may be better equipped to subdue any desires to succumb to the use of stimulants or other drugs.

Name _____ Date _____

REACTIONS

Directions: List the different types of symptoms which might be the result of stimulant abuse under the appropriate headings below.

Physical Symptoms   **Social Symptoms**   **Educational Symptoms**

After you have listed the symptoms, write a paragraph in response to each of the following:

1. How do you determine that a peer is addicted?

2. How do you react to those symptoms?

3. How do you assist an addicted peer?

4. Does the knowledge of these symptoms deter you from using stimulants?

5. Select five of the symptoms that deter you most from using stimulants and grade them from 1 to 5, with 5 being the symptom that you find most disagreeable and would least like to show yourself.

   1.

   2.

   3.

   4.

   5.

6. How would these symptoms interfere with your immediate and future life goals? Answer in at least two paragraphs, one for immediate and one for life goals. Use the back of this page.

Understanding the Harmful Effects of Drug Use

Behavioral Objective: The students will gain an understanding of the harmful effects of drug use, which not only can lead to problems with health, mental ability, and physical fitness, but also can provoke depression to such an extent that it can cause death by overdose with a strong desire for suicide.

Directed Lessons:

1. **Establish the Need:** We are living today in a society that is saturated with pills. There are pills for everything that ails humanity, from headaches to weight loss and for every sickness, real and imagined. Therefore, youth is greatly tempted to use pills for curing their "depressive moods" and to give them an immediate "high" especially when meeting groups of peers who do likewise. Students, therefore, have to learn to understand that many pills, especially those sold only on prescription, are harmful drugs and the serious consequence their excessive and inappropriate use can have on their health, behavior, future and well-being. They will learn that overdosing with drugs will certainly destroy their plans for a successful future and can even lead to death.

2. **Introduction:** The teacher will read this story to the class:

   As students resumed their classes on Monday morning, they were very saddened by the news that one of their classmates had died because of an overdose of drugs. There were extra counselors and volunteers available to try and help the students deal with the loss of one of their peers. As the day went on, they learned more about how their classmate died.

   Judy W. was an attractive and very popular student at the high school. Even with all of this, her friends stated that she had been very unhappy at home, apparently often feeling unloved and unwanted. Following her parents' divorce, Judy went to live with her grandparents, who were unaware of her drug problem and hence had not attempted to help her with it.

   Judy died of an overdose of barbiturates. Her death was classified as an accident because there was no evidence that she intended to take her own life. Actually, it was about as accidental as playing Russian roulette. Judy didn't intentionally take too many pills. She was familiar with them, had taken them before, and knew what to expect. She'd even had an earlier scare from a nonfatal overdose.

   Judy's mind was clouded by the first few pills that she took, then she lost count and eventually ingested a lethal number. She was dying before she swallowed the last pill. Judy had escalated the odds against herself by combining pills with alcohol. Her friends said that she had not been particularly different from other girls

they knew, most of whom also took pills in combination with beer or wine. In Judy's case however, the combination had been lethal. She had not been able to find something that eluded her, but she had ultimately found death.

3. ***Identify the Skill Components:*** Write the following skill components on the board or on a transparency to be used with an overhead projector, or on sentence strips:

   1. Evaluate the situation.
   2. Identify reasons for drug use.
   3. Consider the consequences.
   4. Realize if addiction is present.
   5. Consider other activities of interest.
   6. Decide if you need help.
   7. Decide whom to ask for help.
   8. Look for help from a trusted adult.
   9. Decide on a plan of action.

4. ***Model the Skill:*** The teacher will play the role of a student who had problems and thought that her/his problems could be dealt with by taking drugs. (Problems such as loneliness, depression, etc.) The teacher will use the skill components to model the skill.

5. ***Behavioral Rehearsal:***

   A. *Selection:* The teacher will select three groups of students for role playing. (The number of role plays will depend on the time available for the exercise.)

   B. *Role Play:* Each group of students will be asked by the teacher to role play a situation that relates to the harmful effects caused by drugs. They will use the skill components to role play. The following three role play situations are suggested:

      – Students will exhibit various effects caused by drugs, including: (a) symptoms of delirium, hallucination and manic depression; (b) symptoms of restlessness, nervousness, excitement, insomnia, muscle twitching, and gastrointestinal complaints; and (c) psychological dependency, in which an individual experiences a strong need for a drug whenever he or she feels anxious or tense.

      – Students will exhibit withdrawal symptoms when the drug is unavailable. These are physical symptoms such as sweating, tremors, and tension.

      – Students will role play a desire for overdosing and committing suicide.

   C. *Completion:* After each role play, the teacher will reinforce correct behaviors, identify inappropriate behaviors, and re-enact role play with corrections. If there are no corrections, role play is complete.

   D. *Reinforcers:* The teacher will give verbal and non-verbal praise (specific) for correct behavior.

   E. *Discussion:* The teacher will start a discussion by asking the students the following questions:

- **Can prescription drugs have effects similar to those of illegal drugs?**
- **Should you stop and think before reaching for a bottle of pills?**
- **What have you learned about the serious consequences of drugs?**
- **Could you become addicted after only one try?**
- **How could the first try of drug use affect your future?**
- **If you have already had a "first try," what can you do?**

6. *Practice:* The teacher will distribute copies of the following worksheet, "Harmful Effects of Drugs" and divide the class into groups. The teacher will assign each group a specific drug as the topic for their worksheet: barbiturates, tobacco, alcohol, marijuana, inhalants, cocaine/crack, stimulants, depressants. The group will be asked to list the harmful effects of this drug. One person from each group will be asked to give a brief class presentation about their specific drug and its harmful effects. A class discussion will follow each presentation.

7. *Independent Use:* The teacher will distribute the worksheet "Drugs!" for students to do outside of class. The teacher will ask students to return the completed worksheet in one week to share with the class.

8. *Continuation:* The teacher will remind students periodically of the harmful effects of drugs and that using drugs can be a matter of life or death. The teacher will emphasize that drug use will also seriously affect students' academic performance and, in adult life, their job performance. Whenever possible, the teacher will help the students to conclude that drug use does not solve problems but increases them, limits opportunities for success in the present and future and, in general, destroys lives.

Name _____ Date _____

HARMFUL EFFECTS OF DRUGS

Assigned Drug: _____

List of Harmful Effects:

_____

_____

_____

_____

_____

_____

_____

_____

_____

_____

_____

_____

_____

_____

_____

_____

_____

_____

Name _____   Date _____

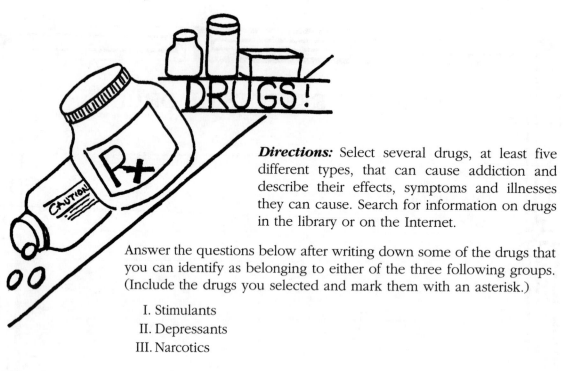

Directions: Select several drugs, at least five different types, that can cause addiction and describe their effects, symptoms and illnesses they can cause. Search for information on drugs in the library or on the Internet.

Answer the questions below after writing down some of the drugs that you can identify as belonging to either of the three following groups. (Include the drugs you selected and mark them with an asterisk.)

  I. Stimulants
 II. Depressants
III. Narcotics

The questions are:

1. Do all drugs have the same effects on body and mind?

2. What are the effects that your selected drugs have?

    a.

    b.

    c.

    d.

    e.

3. What tests are used to measure the presence of drugs in the body?

4. What are the immediate effects of your selected drugs?

    a.

    b.

    c.

    d.

    e.

Drugs! *(cont'd)*

5. What long-term effects, if any, will using these selected drugs have on the body and mind?

    a.

    b.

    c.

    d.

    e.

6. What effect can an overdose of a drug have?

7. Is the above true for all drugs?

8. What are the treatments for drug addiction?

9. Who can help?

Seeking Help to Conquer Drug Addiction

Behavioral Objective: Students will learn that seeking help for drug addiction is the only step to achieving a happier and healthier life, and that most frequently drug addiction can only be conquered by getting help from an officially recognized treatment center.

Directed Lesson:

1. **Establish the Need:** Curious to try anything new or different, young people frequently will be very tempted to experiment with the use of drugs. Even if they decide not to continue, they might not be able to let go since the "first time" try may have already caused them to be addicted without their realizing it immediately. Also, teenagers often get deeper and deeper into drugs and alcohol abuse because they, themselves, and their friends, teachers and parents either pretend that there is no problem or do not know what to do about it. Therefore, the students have to learn not only to recognize their drug addiction but also to know how to seek help and whom to ask for help to conquer their drug addiction and realize that seeking help is the most positive step they can take.

2. **Introduction:** The teacher will read this story to the class:

   Jim and Ashley had been good friends in junior high school, but rarely saw each other in high school. Jim had heard that Ashley was smoking marijuana and using other drugs, but was still shocked when he ran into her at a party.

   It took a few minutes for Ashley to remember who Jim was. She seemed totally spaced out. She told him how out of control she felt and that drugs had taken over her life. Ashley spoke about how she stole things to get money for drugs and how she even had boys pay her for sex. She also told him that she skipped classes a lot and didn't care much about school anymore.

   Jim couldn't get Ashley out of his mind, and he looked for her in the halls and lunchroom. Whenever he saw her, he talked to her and urged her to call the local drug abuse hotline.

   One day, Ashley got so low, she listened to Jim's advice. She found people who listened to her problems without lecturing her. With the help of a counselor, friends like Jim, her parents, and a strong support program, Ashley broke away from her chemical dependency and started regaining control of her life again.

   The teacher asks the class: **How do you think Ashley was able to break away from her chemical dependency?**

3. **Identify the Skill Components:** Write the following skill components on the board or on transparencies to be used with an overhead projector, or on sentence strips:

1. Evaluate the situation.
2. Identify the reasons for drug use.
3. Analyze the pleasures.
4. Analyze the harm to you and others.
5. Define the consequences.
6. Decide if you are addicted to drugs.
7. Decide if you need help.
8. Select a trusted adult to help.
9. Make a plan of action.

4. *Model the Skill:* The teacher will play the role of a student who is addicted to drugs and is now seeking help for his/her problem. The teacher will list the skill components on the board, which he/she is using to role play the student before realizing that finding help is the only positive step to take. The class will then have a discussion about how and when to get help for drug dependence by using the skill components.

5. *Behavioral Rehearsal:*

A. *Selection:* The teacher will choose several groups of students for role playing. (The number of groups will depend on the time available for the exercise.)

B. *Role Play:* The teacher will give each group of students a situation in which they need to seek help for their drug problem. Two role play situations are as follows:

   – Two male students try to help another male student to get help for his dependence problem. (Upon completion of role play, the teacher will switch to female students.)

   – A student feels that he/she has hit bottom, and seeks to find help for conquering drug dependence and discusses his/her problem with an adult.

C. *Completion:* After each role play, the teacher will reinforce correct behaviors, identify inappropriate behaviors, and ask the students to re-enact the role play with corrections. If there are no corrections, role play is complete.

D. *Reinforcers:* The teacher will give verbal and non-verbal praise (specific) for correct behavior.

E. *Discussion:* The teacher will start a discussion by asking the following questions:

   ▶ **Why do you need help when you are addicted to a drug?**
   ▶ **Is it shameful to seek help?**
   ▶ **Is it necessary to seek help?**
   ▶ **Could you conquer drug addiction without help?**
   ▶ **If you have no help, what could happen?**

6. *Practice:* The teacher will distribute copies of the following worksheet, "Seeking Help for Drug Dependence," and ask students to write down three situations they have encountered recently when they knew that someone needed help with a problem relating to some form of drug dependence. They will then choose one of those situations as a scenario for modeling the skill, and suggesting appropriate actions.

7. ***Independent Use:*** The teacher will ask the students to complete the worksheet "Assistance Groups" by listing names and phone numbers of hotlines and drug abuse counseling services. (They usually are listed in the telephone directory under crisis services, alcohol abuse information and treatment, and drug abuse information. Other sources are community and school bulletin boards, libraries, and newspapers.) The students will return the worksheet in one week with all the agencies and phone numbers they found and the teacher will select two students to compose a master list, which will be distributed to each student.

8. ***Continuation:*** The teacher will stress the point that if you have a problem with drug dependence, there are organizations and people to assist you. The teacher will emphasize that it is best to ask for help even after you become an adult since it is almost impossible to conquer drug dependence without professional help.

Name _____ Date _____

SEEKING HELP FOR DRUG DEPENDENCE

I. List three situations you know about when someone needed help with a problem relating to drug dependence.

    1. _____

    2. _____

    3. _____

II. Copy the 9 skill components from the board.

    1. _____

    2. _____

    3. _____

    4. _____

    5. _____

    6. _____

    7. _____

    8. _____

    9. _____

III. Choose one of the situations you listed at the top of the page. Use the skill components and decide how you would assist someone in deciding to seek help for a drug dependence problem.

Name _____ Date _____

ASSISTANCE GROUPS

LOCAL ASSISTANCE GROUPS

NAME   PHONE NUMBER

_____   _____

_____   _____

_____   _____

_____   _____

_____   _____

_____   _____

_____   _____

_____   _____

NATIONAL ASSISTANCE GROUPS

_____   _____

_____   _____

_____   _____

_____   _____

_____   _____

_____   _____

_____   _____

Assessing Friendships

Behavioral Objective: Students will learn to assess "friendships" by recognizing if the friendship is real or dictated by false motivations such as using a "friend" as a scapegoat, as for instance as a stand-in or a lookout after committing an illegal act or behaving inappropriately.

Directed Lesson:

1. **Establish the Need:** Friendship is important to youth, particularly the friendship of peers during their teen years. Therefore, young people are often led into assisting in illegal acts under the guise of friendship. Students need to be able to assess the motivations of others to determine whether or not they are "true friends" and analyze whether or not they will take advantage of their friendship.

2. **Introduction:** The teacher will ask the following questions:

   ▶ **Have you ever been "burned" by someone you thought was a friend? How?**

   ▶ **Would it have been possible to "see it coming"?**

   ▶ **How can you prevent something like this from happening again?**

   ▶ **How do you determine who is a "true friend"?**

   The teacher will read the following story:

   > **Tony is in the restroom between class changes when his new "friend" Ron suddenly runs in from the hall. Ron hands Tony, a good student who has never been in trouble before, a small paper bag rolled up halfway, telling Tony, "Put this in your bookbag for me, man. Some dudes are after me, trying to take my stuff from me. They'll never think you have it. Hurry up, man." Tony hesitates and Ron responds, "Man, you're my friend. I'd help you. Hurry up, man. These guys will be here in a minute. Put it in your bag and get out of here." Tony reluctantly puts the lunchbag in his bookbag and starts out the door, where he bumps into the school security guard who takes Tony and Ron to the office. Both students are searched and crack cocaine is found in the lunchbag Ron gave to Tony. The police are called and Tony is arrested for possession of drugs. Ron leaps out of the office window and the police are unable to catch him at that time.**

   > **What will happen to Tony?**

3. **Identify the Skill Components:** List the following skill components on the board or on sentence strips:

   1. Evaluate your friends objectively.

   2. Assess each situation.

3. Assess possible motivations.

4. Analyze any requested actions.

5. Weigh the risks.

6. Consider alternatives.

7. Make a plan.

8. Do what is best for you.

4. **Model the Skill:** The teacher will model a situation where someone that he/she thinks is a friend actually uses him/her as a "scapegoat" for something that the person did wrong. An example might be that a student who was a "friend" of another student in his/her class tried to use him/her as an excuse with the teacher for not following the rules and regulations of the school and in the classroom.

5. **Behavioral Rehearsal:**

   A. *Selection:* The teacher will ask four students to role play the story in the introduction.

   B. *Role Play:* The teacher will ask the students to role play the four characters (two boys, school safety guard, policeman) portrayed in the introductory story and use the skill components in order to change the story to have a different ending.

   C. *Completion:* After each role play, the teacher corrects the role play and any improper use (or lack of use) of the skill components. If no corrections are needed the role play is complete.

   D. *Reinforcers:* The teacher and peers will compliment the students and thank them with high praise.

   E. *Discussion:* The teacher will lead a class discussion by asking questions such as:

   ▶ **What was Ron's motivation for having Tony as a "friend"?**

   ▶ **What was Tony's motivation for helping Ron?**

   ▶ **Was either a true friend to the other?**

   ▶ **Did Ron evaluate his friendship properly? How should he have acted?**

6. **Practice:** Distribute the worksheet "Friends to the End" and have students complete and discuss it in class.

7. **Independent Use:** Have students take home the worksheet "A Friend Will . . ." and ask them to complete and return it for a future class discussion in one week.

8. **Continuation:** The teacher will use various class, school, or community incidents to highlight "motivations of friends" during the course of the school year, emphasizing the importance of using the skill components to analyze if the friendship can be trusted or is faked and motivated by false motives.

Name _____ Date _____

FRIENDS TO THE END

Directions: Read the following story, then answer the questions below it as they relate to the skill components in this lesson.

Sylvia and Anna were friends for a year. They would hang out together regularly in school and in the neighborhood. They promised each other to be "friends to the end" many times. Over the summer, Sylvia started hanging out with Marla, a new girl who moved on the street, in addition to hanging with Anna. Anna and Marla did not hit it off and clearly did not get along. One day, Sylvia suddenly stopped talking to Anna. Anna, who was quite upset, saw Sylvia walking to school and hanging out the next few weeks with Marla and her brother Scott, who always seemed to be hanging around Sylvia.

1. What sudden change happened in the relationship between Sylvia and Anna?

2. What possible motivation(s) could Sylvia have for her to stop talking to Anna?

3. How should Anna deal with the situation (using the skill components)?

Name _____ Date _____

A FRIEND WILL . . .

Directions: Complete the following statements by using the skill components.

1. A true friend will:

2. A true friend will not:

3. When I decide who is a true friend, I will:

CRIME

Selecting Appropriate Role Models

Behavioral Objective: Students will learn to identify objectively the different behaviors of adults and select appropriate role models to guide them by example in order to learn the behaviors which are necessary for a clean, interesting and productive life both at present and in the future.

Directed Lesson:

1. ***Establish the Need:*** Many young people fail to recognize inappropriate behavior of adults whom they select as role models. This is especially true when the selected person is a family member or an intimate friend of the family who was a guide to the youngster years before this person started participating in anti-social activities. Other youngsters do justify their own social behavior by selecting, purposefully, a role model with bad habits so that they will have an excuse when they are doing something wrong to say that they are following his/her lead. Adopting carefully selected role models with appropriate behaviors will help the students to get a good start for their future success in life.

2. ***Introduction:*** The teacher will ask the following questions for discussion:

   ▶ **How would you select a role model?**

   ▶ **What characteristics do you admire in a person?**

   ▶ **Should you follow a role model blindly or be discerning?**

   ▶ **What kind of a role model would be especially good for you?**

   ▶ **Can you blame a role model for your actions? Is the responsibility yours or can you shift it to another person?**

   The teacher will read the following story:

   Michelle just turned 13 years old. During the past two years, she has watched her brother Ricky, who is 18, join a neighborhood gang and sell crack cocaine. Her parents have worked hard to keep Ricky from getting involved in gang and drug activities, but Michelle knows that he is deep into both areas, even though he has kept it away from their home. Michelle has always "looked up" to Ricky, who has watched over her and protected her as she has grown up.

   One day, on the way home from school, Michelle is approached by Tina. Tina has grown up with Michelle in their neighborhood and she hangs with Ricky and his gang. Tina, who is also 18, has taken Michelle to the mall and to the movies, and let Michelle hang around with her whenever she wanted to. This day, Tina tells Michelle that she wants Michelle to sell "rock" (crack) for her and the gang. Michelle first says "no" but Tina presses the matter, constantly reminding

Michelle that her brother Ricky sells crack and, so, "It can't be all bad." Michelle tells Tina that she will think about it.

Michelle knows that selling drugs is illegal and hanging with the gang can end up getting her into trouble. But she also thinks about Tina and Ricky, whom she has always looked up to all of her life. She thinks: If Ricky and Tina do it, it must not be too bad. If Ricky and Tina do it, it must be o.k. Michelle spends all night wondering what she should do. What do you think she finally decided to do?

Ask students to respond to the following questions:

- **Who are Michelle's role models?**
- **Why did Michelle choose role models that are involved in illegal activities?**
- **Would it be better for Michelle to select a different role model?**
- **What qualities in a role model should Michelle look for?**

3. *Identify the Skill Components:* List the following skill components on the board or on sentence strips:

1. List the good and bad characteristics of the person you want as a role model.
2. Identify the role model's behavior and activity.
3. Decide if the role model is involved in socially acceptable activities that are good for you.
4. Resist peer pressure even from a good friend or family member.
5. Take responsibility for your action.
6. Become accountable to yourself.
7. Analyze your relationship with the person who you consider not worthy to be your role model.
8. Do what is best for you and your future.
9. Make your decision.

4. *Model the Skill:* The teacher will model a story similar to the one in the introduction. The teacher will play the role of Michelle and select a student to be Tina. If the students are boys, change to boy names. The teacher will show how Michelle can use the skill component to reach a decision.

5. *Behavioral Rehearsal:*

A. *Selection:* The teacher selects three students to role play the scenario described in the introduction to this lesson.

B. *Role Play:* The selected students will be asked by the teacher to role play the scenario involving Michelle, Tina, and Ricky. Michelle will apply the skill components to come to a decision.

C. *Completion:* After the role play the teacher will reinforce correct behavior, identify inappropriate behavior, and ask the students to re-enact role play with corrections. If there are no corrections, role play is complete.

D. *Reinforcers:* The teacher and peers will acknowledge correct behavior with verbal praise.

E. *Discussion:* The teacher will lead the discussion by asking the following questions:

- **If you were Michelle or in a similar situation, what would you decide to do?**

- **Is it okay for Michelle to sell crack because her best friend and her beloved brother do so?**

- **If Michelle agrees to sell crack, who would be responsible? What would be the consequences when caught?**

- **Will it help Michelle when caught that Ricky and Tina are in it too?**

6. ***Practice:*** The teacher will hand out copies of the worksheet, "But My _____ Did it, Too!" Students will complete the worksheet, which requires students to identify a situation where he/she did something inappropriate with the excuse that it was done by a family member or friend, too. A discussion in class will follow the completion of the worksheet.

7. ***Independent Use:*** The teacher will distribute copies of the worksheet "Why Should It Be Different for Me?" The worksheet requires the student to research a current news story involving a high profile person in the public eye who has been involved in inappropriate activities and how he/she could avoid getting involved in such a situation. The teacher will ask the students to return the completed worksheets in one week to share them in class for discussion.

8. ***Continuation:*** The teacher will periodically discuss the value of adopting an appropriate role model, how important it is to have a role model who can be trusted and guide the student so that he/she develops into a person with appropriate life (values) skills.

Name _____ Date _____

BUT MY _____ DID IT, TOO!

Directions: Think about a situation where a brother, sister, family member, or close friend did something you knew was inappropriate and asocial. Even though you knew it was wrong, you did the same thing. When you were caught by your parents, a teacher, or another adult, you made an attempt to justify what you did by saying, "But _____ did it, too."

1. Describe such a situation.

2. Should you have selected such a person as a role model?

3. How should you select a role model?

4. Describe the consequences you had to suffer.

5. How did you learn that "But _____ did it, too" is no excuse?

6. How would using the skill components have changed the outcome?

7. How would you act today?

Name _____ Date _____

WHY SHOULD IT BE DIFFERENT FOR ME?

Directions: Research a recent news story involving a well respected person, such as an athlete, politician, or other high profile person in the public eye who participated in an antisocial behavior. Such activity might involve committing a crime, unsportsman-like conduct, or others.

1. Summarize the news story by identifying the person, his/her position, and his/her activities.

2. List the positive contributions made by this person to his/her profession or to society.

3. Although the person had the positive characteristics listed in #2, why did the person commit the asocial act?

4. Were there immediate negative consequence(s) for such behavior?

5. If you were the person described in the story, why should you avoid doing what he/she did?

6. How could the skill components help you to avoid such a situation?

Exercising Responsibility When Using the Media

Behavioral Objective: Students will learn to exercise responsibility when using the media, such as the Internet, TV, etc., in order to avoid getting involved in criminal and violent activities.

Directed Lessons:

1. **Establish the Need:** In today's society, young people are widely using entertainment and educational equipment, such as TV, computers, radio and the Internet. Much of the time, they are without proper supervision. Their parents may not realize the ease with which youngsters can access the vast world of information which is available on the Internet. Some of the information may be inappropriate for the youngsters to experience since it may be extremely indecent and violent and thus encourage criminal activity. The more daring, exciting and violent the material is, the more it seems youth are mesmerized by the visions flashing across the screen. They may want to have similar experiences, which then puts their safety and the safety of others in serious jeopardy. Students need to learn to understand to "tune out" those programs which are pornographic, obscene, violent and criminal in nature and which could lead to harmful consequences if imitated by them.

2. **Introduction:** The teacher will invite students to name various types of media and describe how they enhance their lives and increase their knowledge, and will ask one student to list the answers on the board. Next, the teacher will ask if the media can also have some negative influence on their lives, such as to glorify and encourage the development of unsafe, unhealthy and illegal habits and activities. Again the teacher will ask one student to list the answers on the board. The teacher will then ask the students how they will best use the media and how they would choose their programs.

3. **Identify the Skill Components:** Write the following skill components on the board or on sentence strips.

   1. Be responsible when employing the media.
   2. Select the programs carefully.
   3. Consider what the media has to offer.
   4. Consider time and content.
   5. Define the entertaining and educational programs.
   6. Consider the consequences of listening to those.
   7. Define the indecent and violent programs.
   8. Consider the consequences of listening to those.
   9. Analyze the reasons for these programs to be tempting.

10. Weigh those reasons against the consequences.

11. Consider consequences to exposure.

12. Realize that exposure can lead to imitation and participation.

13. Make a decision best for you and your future.

4. ***Model the Skill:*** The teacher will role play a student who listens to a program on the Internet which tries to sell to the listener participation in a financial pyramid scheme. In the program, the student is promised a large money return on his/her investment when participating in the sale of a certain product. The teacher will tell the students that many persons have been enticed to invest in such schemes and lost all their savings and that, therefore, it is best to tune out such programs in order not to be tempted. The teacher will use the skill components to arrive at this decision.

5. ***Behavioral Rehearsal:***

A. *Selection:* The teacher will select three groups of students for the following role plays:

B. *Role Play:* The students will role play the following situations and show how the use of the skill components could be of help to the young people in finding a solution that is best for them.

   – Mary, age 16, is shy and not very confident in her ability to make friends. She spends a lot of time on the Internet. Recently, she talked with a man on the Internet who has been coaxing her to meet him. He says he is 20 years old and likes quiet girls. He lives in a nearby town. Mary has told her girlfriend Denise about these conversations. Denise is worried about Mary.

   – Carl, age 14, spends hours watching television. He changes channels all the time to find the most exciting and violent stories. He tells two classmates that he thinks it would be neat to do some of the things he sees on TV.

   – While "surfing the net," Dean finds directions on how to make a pipe bomb. Together with a friend, he wants to build one. Dean thinks it might be handy to have such a weapon around.

C. *Completion:* The teacher will decide if the role plays were done correctly and the skill components were used properly. If corrections are needed, the teacher will ask the students to re-enact the role plays. If no corrections are needed, the role play is complete.

D. *Reinforcers:* The teacher and peers will compliment the role playing students and will give specific praise for outstanding performance.

E. *Discussion:* The teacher will start the discussion by asking the following questions:

   ‣ **Why is it so tempting to listen to programs that are violent and indecent?**

   ‣ **Is it not a waste of precious time?**

   ‣ **Is the time best spent in listening to violent and indecent programs or to entertaining and educational programs?**

   ‣ **Why can violent and indecent programs have serious consequences?**

⬥ **Are they tempting because there is not enough excitement in real life?**

⬥ **What other activity would give you the same excitement?**

⬥ **Is the time spent listening to those programs wasted time?**

⬥ **Could the time be used better? How?**

6. ***Practice:*** The teacher will have the students complete the worksheet "Media Time" and share their responses in class.

7. ***Independent Use:*** The teacher will distribute the form "Program Rating Sheet" which students will use at home. The teacher will instruct students to select four TV programs to view, to complete the columns on the form and to return the form to class in one week. Students will share their rating sheets and discuss why they think that these programs should be watched and if not, why not and why they assigned the rating as indicated.

8. ***Continuation:*** The teacher will emphasize the need to be selective when using the media, such as the Internet, TV, etc. and that the topics offered can be very informative, educational and entertaining or extremely harmful, dangerous, violent and indecent. The teacher will caution the students to use the media in productive ways.

Name _____ Date _____

"MEDIA TIME"

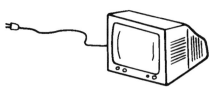

Directions: Select one communications medium and describe how it could be used in a socially productive and efficient manner.

Name _____   Date _____

PROGRAM RATING SHEET

Directions: Select four (4) TV programs to view. After you have seen each program, complete the columns on this sheet and rate the program 1 to 5, with 5 being the best program and 1 being the worst.

Program Name & Length	Brief Description	Entertainment Level	Educational Value	Violence/Indecency Shown

Rating

Distinguishing Between Wants and Needs

Behavioral Objective: Students will learn to be able to distinguish between what they want and what they need to have in life. That means they will learn to discern between items that are desired and those that are necessities for daily life. To acquire this ability is especially important when young people of different financial means meet each other. Students of low and average means might perceive a need for an endless money supply, expensive clothes, and other fashionable items, which they will have to suppress.

Directed Lessons:

1. **Establish the Need:** Many teenagers cannot separate wants from needs in their life. Many youth, especially of low and average means, in order to compete might perceive a need for endless money, expensive and high fashion clothes, cars and other fashionable items. This perceived need, which in reality is a want, often can lead to criminal behavior to obtain these items, i. e., theft, robbery, burglary and other crimes. The ability to distinguish desires from necessities and to realize that life can go on without the desired items is a very important step for students to avoid criminal activities and also to keep students from joining a gang.

2. **Introduction:** The teacher will start a discussion with the following questions:

   ▶ **What items do we <u>need</u> to survive?**

   ▶ **What items do we <u>need</u> to make our life better?**

   ▶ **What things do we <u>want</u> that would make our life more enjoyable, but that we <u>could still live without</u> having?**

   ▶ **What is the risk of getting money by using illegal means?**

   ▶ **Is the risk(s) greater than the gain?**

   ▶ **If a crime is committed to get money, how will it affect your future?**

   The teacher will read the following story:

   Juwan is the second oldest of three children in his family. His father works while his mother takes care of his younger sister. Juwan and the other children live with the parents in an average house, eat regularly, and are provided clothes for school and play. Since money is tight in the household, the family does not go out to eat or to social events. Juwan and the other children have no expensive clothing. While at school, Juwan starts to hang out with students who wear expensive clothes and jewelry, and always have money in their pockets. One of the guys, Tommy, starts making jokes about Juwan's clothes and harasses him in front of the others about never having any money. The other two members of

the group tell Juwan that they know how he can get money so that he can have the same things they have, but he stands the risk of getting busted for doing it. What does Juwan do?

3. ***Identify the Skill Components:*** List the following skill components on the board or on sentence strips:

1. Identify your desires.
2. Identify your needs.
3. Analyze the reason(s) for desires.
4. Identify the risk(s) you have to take to get money by illegal means.
5. Evaluate the consequences.
6. Analyze how the consequences will impact your future.
7. Analyze the gain, if any, you will have for following your desires.
8. Make a wise decision.

4. ***Model the Skill:*** The teacher first lists the following pairs of items on the board:

Needs	Wants
1. casual shoes	1. brand-name athletic shoes
2. warm winter jacket	2. leather jacket with athletic team emblem
3. five-year-old car from father	3. brand-new sports car
4. $75 a week legal income	4. $250 a week income from illegal sources

The teacher will model the skill of this lesson by using the needs and wants he/she has listed on the board (see above) and the skill components to show that it is a wise decision for students to be satisfied if their needs are met and not to consider wants they can only obtain if they resort to illegal actions.

5. ***Behavioral Rehearsal:***

A. *Selection:* The teacher will select three groups of four students to play Juwan and his friends.

B. *Role Play:* The teacher will ask each group to role play the modeled skill using the skill components.

C. *Completion:* After the role play, the teacher will reinforce correct behavior, identify inappropriate behavior, and ask the students to re-enact the role play with corrections. If there are no corrections, role play is complete.

D. *Reinforcers:* The teacher will compliment the students for their participation in performing the role play. In some cases, the teacher will ask the students who did not participate in the role plays to select the best performing group and the teacher will give special praise to this group.

E. *Discussion:* Students and teacher will discuss the differences between desires and necessities in the role play and in life. The teacher will point out that at all times in life there exist unfulfilled desires, not only during their life as students. Therefore, learning to live without some desired items is necessary and has to be accepted.

6. ***Practice:*** The teacher will distribute the worksheet "Wants and Needs" to students to complete and discuss in class.

7. ***Independent Use:*** The teacher will hand out the worksheet "Interview Guide" and ask the students to interview a few of their friends or siblings (not classmates) who are teenagers and ask them to identify their needs and wants and how they would distinguish between needs and wants and what they would do to obtain them or if they would decide to go without them. The teacher will also ask the students to complete the last column of the "Interview Guide" and then return the fully completed guide in one week for discussion in class.

8. ***Continuation:*** The teacher will continue to point out that needs are different from wants and identify how students can compromise when they cannot get everything they want. Students should learn that being without certain items they desire is better than the consequences they would experience for fulfilling all their desires by employing illegal means.

Name _____   Date _____

WANTS AND NEEDS

Directions: Name six wants and needs you perceive as necessities for you, and the reasons why you consider them as such. Then list the wants and needs in priority order and indicate which items are a "must," which are on the "borderline," and which you can let go and live without. Use the skill components whenever they are applicable.

WANTS

1. _____
2. _____
3. _____
4. _____
5. _____
6. _____

NEEDS

1. _____
2. _____
3. _____
4. _____
5. _____
6. _____

REASON FOR WANTS

1. _____
2. _____
3. _____
4. _____
5. _____
6. _____

REASON FOR NEEDS

1. _____
2. _____
3. _____
4. _____
5. _____
6. _____

		"Must"	"Borderline"	"Will Do Without"
WANTS:	1. _____			
	2. _____			
	3. _____			
	4. _____			
	5. _____			
	6. _____			
NEEDS:	1. _____			
	2. _____			
	3. _____			
	4. _____			
	5. _____			
	6. _____			

Name _____ Date _____

INTERVIEW GUIDE

Interviewer _____ Date _____
(student)

Interviewees _____
(relations)

Directions: Ask the interviewees what needs and wants they have in life. List 5 or more needs and wants in the first column and list in the second column what the interviewees would do to obtain these needs and wants or if they would rather do without them. State in the third column what you would do and what decision you would make about the same needs and wants and which skill components you used to make your decision.

Needs	What would interviewees do to obtain the needs and wants or to do without them?	What would you do and which skill components would you use to make your decision?
Wants		

Dealing with "Appetite" for Illegal Activities

Behavioral Objective: Students will learn to deal with their appetite to engage in illegal activities to experience the extremes of excitement. They will learn to understand the reasons for their craving of thrills and realize that illegal activities will lead to incarceration with consequent curtailment of future professional ambitions, while legal activities can provide equally exciting thrills with less severe consequences.

Directed Lesson

1. **Establish the Need:** Young people often find involvement in illegal and antisocial activity exciting, creating an ongoing need for the "rush" they get from illegal activities such as fighting rival gang members, stealing cars, selling drugs, being chased by police and similar activity. The need for this "rush" can lead youth at an accelerated rate toward incarceration or even death. Incarceration might not only be damaging but may destroy the students' dreams for a successful future. Students will be able to learn to fulfill their need for the "rush" by finding legal activities to substitute for the illegal ones.

2. **Introduction:** The teacher will read the following story to the class:

   Alfonso and Raul joined a neighborhood gang about one year ago. After they first joined, they went along with two of their friends to an area suburb where they stole a car from the parking lot of a shopping mall. As Raul pulled the car out of the parking space, the owner saw them and ran to the car. Alfonso knocked the man down, got in the car, and they took off out of the lot. A policeman spotted them about a half mile away from the mall and began chasing the car. Raul drove back into the city with several police cars in pursuit. Raul and Alfonso stopped the car, jumped out and escaped into the neighborhood. Although they were tired, both felt their adrenaline rushing as they enjoyed the thrill of the chase.

   Over the rest of the year, Alfonso and Raul continued to steal cars from various parking lots and driveways. They increased their exploits from two a month to eight or ten stolen cars a month. Not only did they enjoy the "rush" from nearly being caught several times, they also made some money using several fellow gang members to sell car parts of the stolen cars.

   After a year, Alfonso and Raul felt the "rush" somewhat go away. One of their fellow gang members suggested a new spin: carjacking. He told them they would not only get the car, but also all of the money and belongings of its driver. All they needed to do, he told them, was to pack a gun, threaten the driver, take the keys, property, and car. They began thinking about this as a new source of both money and filling their need for excitement that was lost in stealing cars from lots and homes.

The teacher will ask the class:

> ▶ **What are the positive values that Alfonso and Raul think they will receive when they carjack autos by threatening the driver.**

3. *Identify the Skill Components:* List the following skill components on the board or on sentence strips:

1. Analyze if craving for "thrills" is the reason for the desire to commit illegal acts.

2. Analyze also if this was the reason for joining a gang.

3. Identify the consequences resulting from illegal activity.

4. Analyze why you crave "thrills" and excitement.

5. Decide if this craving is due to other needs such as belonging, showing off, etc.

6. Identify legal activities to satisfy your appetite for excitement.

7. Select an appropriate social group and a legal activity.

8. Participate in such a group and activity.

4. *Model the Skill:* The teacher will role play why he/she craves thrills and how a legal activity he/she considers exciting can satisfy the needs. It could be sky diving, sail flying, skiing, rock climbing, etc. The teacher will show how satisfying such activity can be and bring the same thrills that are derived from entertaining illegal activities and have less severe consequences. The teacher will use the skill components to show why he/she prefers a legal activity to satisfy her/his appetite for thrills.

5. *Behavioral Rehearsal:*

A. *Selection:* The teacher will select two students to role play and will select further pairs of students if time permits further role play.

B. *Role Play:* The teacher will ask the students to role play the story in the introduction with Alfonso and Raul going to the suburban shopping mall with the intent of stealing a car. The two students will role play what Alfonso and Raul think and say about considering stealing the car. Using the skill components during the role play, the students will select legal activities and proceed to participate in those activities, bringing about a comparable excitement.

C. *Completion:* The teacher will decide if the role play was done correctly and the skill components were used correctly. If corrections are needed, the teacher will ask the students to re-enact the role play.

D. *Reinforcers:* The teacher will praise the students for their role play and ask the whole class to applaud.

E. *Discussion:* The teacher will start a discussion by asking the following questions:

> ▶ **Why did Alfonso and Raul join a gang?**

> ▶ **What are the consequences that Alfonso and Raul had to face when caught?**

> ▶ **Could there be consequences which would destroy the goals they set for themselves in life?**

▶ **What legal activities could they have chosen to get the "rush" and "thrill" they seem to crave?**

6. ***Practice:*** The teacher will divide the class into groups of two. He/she will ask each group to complete the worksheet "Packin' and Jackin,'" then discuss their answers in class.

7. ***Independent Use:*** The teacher will distribute the worksheet "Thrills and Chills" for students to complete as a homework assignment. The teacher will ask the students to return the completed worksheets in one week for discussion in class.

8. ***Continuation:*** The teacher will emphasize the importance of selecting legal sources of excitement and reiterate the potential consequences of doing illegal activities. The teacher will continue to use examples of incidents occurring at school and in the community where youth choose legal activities as a source of satisfaction rather than illegal activities. The teacher will, when appropriate, work with students in groups and one-on-one to identify their areas of interest and assist them to find means to achieve the excitement they crave through pursuit of legal activities.

Name _____ Date _____

PACKIN' AND JACKIN'

Directions: Using the story in the introduction, answer the following questions by applying the skill components.

1. In the minds of Alfonso and Raul, what do they think they are getting out of carjacking?

2. Why do they crave excitement?

3. List the consequences that could occur from their carjacking. (For example: What would they do if the driver resisted? What if the driver had a gun? What if the police catch them?)

4. What legal activities could Alfonso and Raul do that would provide a similar level of excitement without the risks associated with the illegal activity of stealing cars or carjacking?

5. What should a student do if an activity ceases to provide the level of excitement he or she wants to experience?

Name _____ Date _____

 # Thrills and Chills

Directions: Complete the page below by listing five legal activities that you would like to do that would bring excitement ("thrills") to you. Then list five ways you relax or enjoy yourself ("chills"). Next to each thrill and chill, give a brief explanation of why you would enjoy doing each activity.

THRILLS

1.

2.

3.

4.

5.

CHILLS

1.

2.

3.

4.

5.

Realizing that Consequences for Criminal Acts Are Unavoidable

Behavioral Objective: Students will learn that there is little chance to avoid consequences when committing a crime.

Directed Lesson:

1. **Establish the Need:** Students often believe that they can avoid consequences for committing a criminal act by using devious means. However, students will learn that even if they are lucky enough not to be caught by the police the first time they commit a criminal act, they will be eventually caught and then suffer severe consequences. Their consequences can affect their well-being through their entire life because they might become physically crippled and mentally affected, spend years in detention or prison, and have a permanent criminal record which will make it impossible to prepare for their employment careers of choice.

2. **Introduction:** The teacher will ask the following questions:

   ▶ **What is a crime?**
   ▶ **Why would anyone want to do it?**
   ▶ **What is the reason or objective for doing it?**
   ▶ **Is it worth doing it when considering the consequences?**
   ▶ **What are the chances of being caught?**
   ▶ **Does it matter if it's the first time or the fourth time?**
   ▶ **What is meant by "mentally affected"?**

   The teacher will emphasize that no criminal can escape forever the consequences of paying for crimes they commit.

   The teacher will then read the following story:

   Bobby and Carlos had been hanging out with a group of neighborhood friends for almost a year. Several members of the group were known to steal cars and break into houses. Bobby and Carlos were asked to go along to steal cars several times. Bobby did not go the first two times but eventually went along on five occasions. Carlos did not go any of these times and stayed behind with the others.

   One Friday night, Bobby pressed Carlos to go along on a home burglary. Bobby hassled Carlos for an hour, explaining that he (Bobby) had helped steal three cars and break into two houses over the past six months, and that he was never caught once. Carlos eventually gave in and went along.

211

The group rode in a stolen car to a house about a mile away. They broke a basement window and all four went inside the house. As they walked up the basement stairs to the first floor, a door opened and the homeowner pointed a gun at Carlos. Carlos was scared and pushed past the owner to run out a nearby back door. The gun went off and Carlos was struck in the chest.

Meanwhile, Bobby and the other two friends ran back into the basement and climbed out the broken window, then ran through neighborhood streets, where they were caught and arrested by the police three blocks away from the scene of the crime. Carlos was hospitalized and required surgery to remove a lung. All four individuals were later convicted in juvenile court and sentenced to two years in a state facility for being in possession of stolen property and for the burglary.

Ask students to respond to the following questions:

▶ How did Bobby persuade Carlos to go along with the group?

▶ What consequences did Bobby and Carlos face for their criminal act?

▶ What was the difference between Bobby's and Carlos's situations?

3. *Identify the Skill Components:* List the following skill components on the board or on sentence strips:

1. Consider the consequences to yourself for committing a criminal act.
2. Consider the consequences to the victim and their families.
3. Ask yourself if it is worth the risk.
4. Consider the likelihood of being caught.
5. Consider the possibility of being hurt.
6. Consider how this will affect your future.
7. Think of your ambitions for the future.
8. Think of ways to resist peer pressure, if applied.
9. Make a wise choice.

4. *Model the Skill:* The teacher will model the skill with one student using the story in the introduction. The teacher will role play Carlos with the student playing the role of Bobby trying to persuade "Carlos" to participate in the group's activity. The teacher as Carlos will use the skill components to show how to resist the pressure from Bobby to make him a participant in the criminal activity.

5. *Behavioral Rehearsal:*

A. *Selection:* The teacher selects two pairs of students.

B. *Role Play:* The teacher asks both pairs to role play a scenario similar to that in the introduction, but with these reservations:

– The two students of the first pair have participated in stealing a car on two other occasions as members of a group and have not been caught before.

— The two students of the second pair have never participated in criminal acts with or without a group and have been pressured by peers to do so.

C. *Completion:* The teacher and peers will analyze the role play and the use of the skill components and the teacher will ask the students to re-enact the role play if corrections are necessary. If no corrections are needed, the role play is complete.

D. *Reinforcers:* The teacher will compliment the students for their participation in the role play. In some cases, the teacher will ask the students who did not participate who they think was the best performing group and give special praise to that group.

E. *Discussion:* Students will discuss the following questions:

   ▶ **What factors influenced the decision-making process of both groups?**

   ▶ **What difficulties did the students have in making their decision?**

   ▶ **How did the skill components help them come to a decision?**

   ▶ **Did the consequences affect their decision?**

6. ***Practice:*** The teacher will hand out copies of the worksheet "Nothing Is Going to Happen?" for students to complete and discuss in class. The worksheet asks for three situations which led to unavoidable consequences.

7. ***Independent Use:*** The teacher will distribute copies of the worksheet entitled "Play It Out" for students to complete at home, to discuss with their family members, and to bring back to school within a week to discuss with the class.

8. ***Continuation:*** The teacher will continue in upcoming class discussions to identify consequences for committing crimes and point out that even though there may be no immediate consequence, eventually there will be consequences which must be faced.

Name _____ Date _____

NOTHING IS GOING TO HAPPEN?

Directions: List three situations that happened to you, if possible of a serious nature, where you expected to avoid the consequences for your actions but had to face them. List the consequences and explain how they were related to your actions. Tell why these consequences could not be avoided though you tried to avoid them.

SITUATION #1 _____

_____

Consequences: _____

_____

_____

Why the consequences could not be avoided: _____

_____

_____

SITUATION #2 _____

_____

Consequences: _____

_____

_____

Why the consequences could not be avoided: _____

_____

_____

SITUATION #3 _____

_____

Consequences: _____

_____

_____

Why the consequences could not be avoided: _____

_____

_____

Name _____ Date _____

PLAY IT OUT

Read the story started below. Complete the story and write down what you think Latrice should do. Use the skill components.

Latrice was approached by two of her friends, Monique and Jennifer, after her first period class. Jennifer told Latrice that she and Monique were going to cut school for the rest of the day to go to the mall and shoplift some clothes and jewelry. She asked Latrice to join them. What should Latrice do?

Coping with Serious Consequences

Behavioral Objective: Students will develop an awareness of, and an ability to deal with, the serious consequences arising from their behaviors and actions. This may help prevent seemingly insurmountable problems that might cause them to do something out of anger or frustration, which is even worse and thus might lead to more serious consequences than the problems themselves.

Directed Lesson:

1. **Establish the Need:** Teenagers, like adults, are frequently faced with problems or situations which seem insurmountable. These are problems which might not only have an effect on them at present, but might cause a change in their entire life ambitions. The problems can be the result of a death in the family, an overdose of a stimulant, sickness, accident, pregnancy, and so on. Students will learn how to deal with such problems and realize that the best course is to avoid them whenever possible.

2. **Introduction:** The teacher reads the following scenario to the class:

   John is a nineteen-year-old college student who is attending college as a freshman. In high school, as a senior, he was popular among his peers. He owned many material things such as video games, entertainment, a personal stereo and TV as well as a sports car. As a result, he was a "friend" to many of his classmates, especially the girls. During his senior year, he drank heavily "with the group" and earned marginal grades. He did not make thorough plans about attending college, but his father who was a college graduate and successful businessman, had every expectation that his son would succeed in college and do well in later life.

   As a freshman, John was marginally "making the grade." His experience in trying to make new friends was through the "partying circuit." One of his girlfriends was Jill, whom he met at a fraternity party. They had spent many intimate times with each other during the first quarter—to the detriment of their studies. Near the end of the first quarter, their relationship has "cooled" and on a couple of occasions, she was seen with another friend, Jeff. One day John received a "personal and confidential" letter in the mail. As he opened it, he read that Jill was pregnant and she was about to inform her parents that John was the father.

   Immediately thereafter, John met with Jill and an argument ensued. Little was resolved since John had drunk excessively before their meeting. One of the contentions was that John had expressed his disdain of Jeff and with his relationship with Jill.

In nearly a stupor, John returned to his dorm room, drank a fifth of vodka, and slashed his wrists with a razor. He was found in the early evening by his room-mate who had returned to the room from a study session in the library.

3. ***Identify the Skill Components:*** Write the following skill components on the board or on sentence strips:

   1. Analyze the situation.
   2. Define the seriousness of the problem.
   3. Consider that anger is no solution.
   4. Consider possible solutions.
   5. Consider all consequences.
   6. Discuss the solutions with those involved.
   7. Accept your responsibility.
   8. Refrain from using excuses.
   9. Seek the advice of a trusted friend.
   10. Make a rational decision.
   11. Follow through with appropriate action.

4. ***Model the Skill:*** The teacher will role play a student who tried some stimulant, such as cocaine, alcohol or even heroin and show how this student got more and more addicted and dependent and needed greater and greater amounts of money to feed his addiction. The teacher will show how angry the student got with himself but that this anger was no help or solution and that the student finally started to "toy" with the idea to commit suicide. By using the skill components, the teacher will then show how the student can solve his/her problems.

5. ***Behavioral Rehearsal:***

   A. *Selection:* The teacher will select two pairs of students to role play.

   B. *Role Play:* The teacher will ask each pair of students to role play one of the following situations:

      – Bruce, a student who becomes irate and aggressive with Sarah after he learns that his "girlfriend" Sarah has been "running" with Michael, a track star.

      – Sarah, a student who has been dating Michael while "playing along" with Bruce.

      If time permits, the teacher will select one or more pairs of students to role play John and Jill in the situation described in the Introduction.

   C. *Completion:* As each role play is finished, the teacher will determine if the role play was appropriately done. If not, the teacher will ask the students to re-enact the role play with corrections. If yes, the role play is complete.

   D. *Reinforcers:* The teacher will acknowledge his/her appreciation for the efforts and cooperation of the role players and give all actors high praise.

E. *Discussion:* The teacher will solicit comments from the class related to the story in the introduction and their perceptions as to what could have been done by John. The teacher might also start a discussion about the situation in the other role plays.

6. ***Practice:*** The teacher will ask the students to complete the following worksheet, entitled "Insurmountable," and discuss their entries in class.

7. ***Independent Use:*** The teacher will have each student research a newspaper article involving an incident related to out-of-control anger because the problem seemed insurmountable, and write a brief statement as to how the incident could have been resolved in a logical and peaceful manner and by using the skill components.

The students will turn in their reports in one week and discuss them in class.

8. ***Continuation:*** The teacher will continually reinforce that "out of control" anger is an emotion that frequently occurs when any of us is confronted with a problem that seems unsolvable. The teacher will highlight logical solutions to incidents involving such problems.

Name _____ Date _____

INSURMOUNTABLE

Directions: Answer each item below in complete sentences or paragraphs. Use the skill components.

1. List two insurmountable problems that would make you "out-of-control" angry.

    a. _____

    b. _____

2. Why does a seemingly insurmountable problem make you frequently angry?

3. Does such "out-of-control" anger solve the problems?

4. Why not?

5. How did you bring yourself back into control?

6. How did you solve the insurmountable problems?

    a. _____

    b. _____

7. Could the situations have been handled differently?

    a. _____

    b. _____

8. Explain how.

    a. _____

    b. _____

9. Could the problems have been avoided?

    a. _____

    b. _____

10. How ?

    a. _____

    b. _____

11. Did the use of the skill components help you to come to an acceptable solution?

12. Name the skill components that you used.

    a. _____

    b. _____

Learning How to Prevent Date Rape

Behavioral Objective: Students will learn to differentiate between intimacy, conceptual sex and date rape; and how to protect themselves from date rape and avoid situations which could lead to date rape.

Directed Lesson:

1. **Establish the Need:** Often young people do not realize how quickly the fun of dating can turn violent when one or the other does not respect the standards of intimacy and not only demands sex but overpowers the partner to force the act of sex. Not only does date rape result in a traumatic experience, it is a violent and criminal act and should be reported immediately to the proper authorities. Students need to learn how to express and discuss their dating expectations and personal standards in an open and honest manner with their dating partner. Such discussions will help to clarify where one stands on certain dating behaviors, will help to avoid misunderstandings and could lessen the risk of date rape.

2. **Introduction:** The teacher will tell the following story to the class:

   A Grand Opening Dance is being held at the new community center. Since Susan helped with the elementary kids after-school craft classes, she received an invitation to the dance for herself and a guest. Susan really loves to dance, but was not dating anyone at this time; she wondered whom she could ask to go with her. Then she remembered a new boy in school, Bob; he was two grades ahead of her, but was in her study hall. He seemed nice, but it didn't look as though he had made many friends yet. Susan thought it might be nice to ask him; maybe this would help him meet some other kids from school.

   When Susan asked Bob, he immediately said yes, adding that he, too, liked to dance.

   The night of the dance, Bob picked Susan up in his car. He told Susan she really looked terrific, and she did! She had done her hair up which made her look a little older and her new dress was short and tight, which was a popular style among many girls. Susan and Bob were having a great time dancing and mingling with a few of Susan's friends. Then Bob suggested that they leave a little early because he was hungry and thought they could get a bite to eat at this little place he knew outside of town. Susan said "O.K." and they left. Soon after leaving the city limits, Bob pulled off the road onto a side road and stopped the car. Susan asked why he had stopped and Bob said so that they could talk and get to know each other better. But, to Susan's dismay, there wasn't much talk, but a lot of sexual advances. Susan told Bob she really wasn't interested in having sex with him because she didn't know him well enough and that she felt she was really too young. Bob seemed not to hear what Susan was saying and continued to force himself on her. Susan began to cry. Bob told her to shut-up and said that she looked like a big girl and should act like one and enjoy herself.

The teacher will use the following questions to discuss the story:

▶ **Would you say that what happened was date rape?**

▶ **How did Susan get herself into this situation?**

▶ **Was there anything she could have done differently?**

▶ **Who is the guilty party? Why?**

3. ***Identify the Skill Components:*** Write the following skill components on the board or on sentence strips.

1. Date friends you know.
2. Arrange for a double date, if possible.
3. Discuss your relationship before the date.
4. Show respect for each other's wishes.
5. Consider location and activity.
6. Avoid isolation.
7. Show common interest.
8. Avoid provocation.
9. Plan how to leave an uncomfortable situation.
10. Remain alert and under control.

4. ***Model the Skill:*** The teacher will portray Susan in the above story. Using the skill components, the teacher will show how Susan could have avoided a date-rape situation. (There are several occasions in the story where application of the skill components could have changed the outcome.)

5. ***Behavioral Rehearsal:***

A. *Selection:* The teacher will select pairs of students as needed to enact the following role play.

B. *Role Play:* The teacher will have the following role play on index cards, one to be given to each pair of students. Students will decide how to apply the skill components to avoid a date-rape incident. More than one scenario can be role played by the different groups of students.

– Brittany is 15 and her boyfriend Max is 16. Max has brought up the subject of sex several times, but Brittany has always said she was not ready. Brittany and Max are at a party at a friend's house; the parents are gone on an overnight trip. There is alcohol available and some of the couples have left the group and have gone into the bedrooms. Max is insisting that they, too, look for some place so that they can have more "privacy." What is Brittany going to do?

C. *Completion:* After each role play, the teacher will identify inappropriate behaviors, and ask the students to re-enact the role play with corrections, if necessary. If correct, the role play is complete.

D. *Reinforcers:* The teacher and the students will acknowledge the well done performance of the role players and praise them highly.

E. *Discussion:* The teacher will encourage the students to discuss any similar dating situations that they have experienced and how they handled it. The teacher will ask how the skill components could have helped them to diffuse the situations or, better yet, to avoid the complications.

6. **Practice:** The teacher will ask the students to complete the worksheet as "True or False?" After completion, the answers will be discussed in class.

7. **Independent Use:** The teacher will ask the students to write a story of an "ideal date." Students should be very specific in describing the details of such a date. Stories should be returned to class for sharing and discussion in one week.

8. **Continuation:** The teacher will point out that becoming adept in this skill will make it easier for them to avoid violence in their dating relationships. He/she should remind students that open communication and respect for each other's feelings are the best foundations for building loving relationships and enduring friendships.

Name _____ Date _____

TRUE OR FALSE?

1. T   F   Girls say no, but they mean yes.

2. T   F   Young women want a young man who is always in control.

3. T   F   Young people learn certain behaviors from their families and often these behaviors carry over to their relationships.

4. T   F   The three statements above can be used as an excuse for date rape.

5. T   F   It's all right to threaten a person as long as you don't hurt them physically.

6. T   F   You cannot bring charges for date rape if you agreed to go out together.

7. T   F   It's best to find out all of the information you can about your partner before you start dating.

8. T   F   If you don't have sex, you won't be able to hold on to a boy/girl-friend.

9. T   F   No one should know what goes on in a relationship but the two people involved.

10. T   F   It's all right to nag someone until they do what you want them to do.

11. T   F   Females as well as males can be responsible for date rape.

12. T   F   When your date dresses in a certain way, it's an open invitation for sex.

13. T   F   It's all right to touch a person without their permission, just don't have sex.

14. T   F   If my father/mother did it, it's OK for me. If my mother/father accepted it, it's OK for me to accept.

15. T   F   If a guy spends money on a date with you, he is entitled to have sex with you.

16. T   F   Females and males are equal partners.

17. T   F   Females and males should show respect for each other.

18. T   F   A date rape is always the fault of the boy.

19. T   F   Provocation for date rape might come from either partner.

20. T   F   Date rape is a criminal act.

Describe which skill components are most important after you have responded to the items above. Explain why you think they are most important. (Use the back of this page.)

TRUE OR FALSE?

Answer Key

1. F	6. F	11. T	16. T
2. T	7. T	12. F	17. T
3. T	8. F	13. F	18. F
4. F	9. F	14. F	19. T
5. F	10. F	15. F	20. T

Realizing That Guns Do Not Assure Safety

Behavioral Objective: Students will learn that if they encounter situations where they are physically threatened, guns cannot assure their safety but will only aggravate the situation and could cause severe consequences for all involved, including themselves. If they cannot resolve the matter safely, they should ask for and accept help from an adult.

Directed Lesson:

1. **Establish the Need:** Often young people feel threatened or bullied for money, power, or just for fun. Therefore, teens need to learn to determine the seriousness of the situation or remarks and how to safely resolve or deal with the matter. They need to learn how and to whom to go for help when needed. They also must learn that threatening with a gun is never a solution; the presence of guns can only make the situation worse. Using a gun even when only to threaten an adversary can result in you becoming the victim.

2. **Introduction:** The teacher will share the following story with the class:

   For the last two months Brutus, the school bully, has been threatening to beat up Sam. Sam has been able to avoid Brutus by not staying after school and walking home with his older brother Cornell. However, today Sam was late for math class and was given a detention to be served tomorrow after school. Brutus told Sam that tomorrow was going to be "the day" unless Sam would give him $50.00. When Sam and Cornell were walking home the other day, Cornell was excited because he had been promoted to junior assistant at his job beginning tomorrow. He said he had received an early release pass from the principal and would leave school one hour before the end of the school day. Sam was scared to death. He knew that he could never stand up to fighting with Brutus and he didn't have $50.00. Sam thought if he got his father's gun and took it to school with him, he could pull it out and threaten Brutus and then Brutus would leave him alone.

   The teacher will ask the following questions of the class:

   ◗ **Why did Sam make the choice to bring a gun to threaten Brutus?**
   ◗ **What consequences could he face by taking his father's gun to school?**
   ◗ **Did Sam have other choices?**

3. **Identify the Skill Components:** List the following skill components on the board or on sentence strips.

   1. Consider the situation.
   2. Decide the seriousness of the situation.
   3. Think about your options.

4. Define the consequences.

5. Decide if you can safely solve it alone.

6. If you need help, decide whom to ask.

7. Follow through on your decision.

4. **Model the Skill:** The teacher will role play Sam in the story from the introduction. The teacher could use the "think aloud" method to show how Sam could use the skill components to solve this problem. Or, the teacher could ask a student to enact the part of Sam's brother and the two brothers could discuss the problem and decide on a plan by using the skill components.

5. **Behavioral Rehearsal:**

   A. *Selection:* The teacher will select two pairs of students to role play.

   B. *Role Play:* Both pairs of students will role play the story from the introduction or a similar story which they might have experienced themselves. If they role play the story in the introduction, one pair of students can represent Sam and Brutus, while the second pair may portray Sam and his brother Cornell. Both pairs of students will be asked by the teacher to use the skill components to arrive at an appropriate solution with safety in mind.

   C. *Completion:* The teacher will identify incorrect behaviors and ask the students to redo the role plays with corrections if necessary. If there are no corrections, the role play is complete.

   D. *Reinforcers:* The teacher and peers will thank the students for their performance in role playing this critical situation extremely well.

   E. *Discussion:* The teacher will ask the students to discuss what they or someone they know should do in a situation similar to Sam's, especially when they are threatened with physical harm, extortion, and so on. The teacher will make sure that the students weigh the pros and cons of each solution suggested. The teacher will ask the students how the skill components could help them in the future.

6. **Practice:** Distribute copies of the worksheet "Threats" for students to complete and share in class.

7. **Independent Use:** The teacher will distribute copies of the worksheet "Danger" to complete at home. This worksheet directs students to ask family members, relatives or a family friend if they have ever experienced dangerous threats to their well-being and how they dealt with the situation. If the students cannot find someone with whom to share such an experience, they can search for a situation in a newspaper or magazine where threats resulted in physical harm. The students will then describe what they would have done in the same situation. The teacher will request that the students return their completed worksheet within a week to discuss it in class.

8. **Continuation:** The teacher will remind students that threats of physical harm can occur anytime, anywhere throughout their life. That is why it is important to learn how to deal with such situations without turning to guns as a solution. The teacher will emphasize that threatening with a gun will not solve problems but will make them worse. He/she will suggest to the students that remaining calm, thinking through the situation, and applying the skill components could result in a plan which provides safety for all concerned.

Name _____   Date _____

"THREATS"

Directions: Write about a situation (real or made up) in which some-one threatened to harm you or extort money from you. Tell how you handled the situation at the time; then explain how you would handle the situation now using the skill components.

The Situation:

At that time I . . .

Now I would . . .

Name _____ Date _____

"DANGER"

Directions: Interview your parents, relatives or a family friend to learn if they have ever experienced a dangerous threat to their well-being. Describe the situation and how they were able to deal with it. If you cannot find someone with whom to share such an experience, look for a dangerous situation in a newspaper story or magazine article and explain how it was handled and how you would handle it now.

The Dangerous Situation:

How it was handled:

How I would handle it now:

Learning to Respect Guns and Weapons

Behavioral Objective: Students will learn to understand that using guns is never a solution to a problem. Guns are not toys and can cause severe bodily harm and often death. Students will learn to control their urge or curiosity to handle a gun and not to pick up a gun if they find one.

Directed Lesson:

1. **Establish the Need:** Every day in America, about 20 children ages 19 and under are killed by guns through accidental shootings, homicides, and suicides. Many more are wounded or severely injured for life. Because many households are in possession of guns of various types and because guns are readily available through simple sales transactions, both legal and illegal, many youngsters are attracted and have access to guns to play with, hunt with, use for "protection" and even for criminal purposes. Students need to learn to understand the implications that can arise when using a gun and that having a gun may be illegal depending on state laws pertaining to types of guns, age of the gunholder, storage of guns, etc.

2. **Introduction:** The teacher will ask the following questions and list students' answers to some of the questions on the board.

   ▶ **Why do you think people, possibly also your parents, want to own guns?**
   ▶ **Who among you wants to possess a gun?**
   ▶ **Do you know how to get or buy a gun?**
   ▶ **How should guns be stored?**

   Then the teacher will read the following story:

   One Saturday afternoon Mark, who is 12 years old, was tired of watching TV and decided that he wanted to play "Cops and Robbers." He ran upstairs to his 6-year-old brother Steve's room. Steve was playing quietly with some blocks and toy cars. Mark said, "Steve, come play with me. I want to play a Cop who catches the bad guy. You can be the bad guy." At first Steve said "no" but Mark threatened to beat him up if he did not play, so finally Steve agreed and ran downstairs where they were going to play. Mark thought that it would be neat to have a real gun so he tiptoed into his parents' room, went to his father's dresser, and took out the gun that he knew his father kept there.

   Mark and Steve ran through the house playing, yelling, and having a great time until Mark finally cornered Steve. Mark said, "Stick 'em up!" and Steve raised his hands in the air. As he said "Stick 'em up!" Mark pulled the gun out of his pants pocket and pointed it at Steve. "Bang, bang," he said. Steven laughed and said, "You missed." As Mark pointed the gun at Steve again it accidentally fired, hitting

Steve in the chest and killing him instantly. Their father, who had been working in his basement workshop, heard the shot and came running upstairs. He found Mark standing over Steve, crying and shouting over and over again, "Get up now!"

Following the story, the teacher might ask the following questions:

▶ **How many of you have heard of a similar gun-related accidental shooting?**

▶ **How do you think Mark, or any other person holding a gun after it went off, feels?**

▶ **How do you think the father and owner of the gun feels?**

▶ **What are the legal consequences of a situation like the one in the story?**

3. ***Identify the Skill Components:*** Write the following skill components on the board or on sentence strips:

1. Remember that a gun is a powerful weapon.

2. Realize that special training is needed to handle a gun safely.

3. Understand that guns are not toys.

4. Understand that guns do not solve problems.

5. Realize that anyone can become the victim of a gunshot.

6. Think about the serious consequences that could result from handling a gun.

7. If you find a gun, report it and do not handle it.

8. Choose activities that do not involve guns.

9. Think safety first.

4. ***Model the Skill:*** The teacher will play the part of Mark in the preceding story up to the point where Mark goes to his father's dresser to get the gun. He/she will show how the outcome of this story could have been different by using the skill components.

5. ***Behavioral Rehearsal:***

A. *Selection:* The teacher will select 4–5 students for the first role play and 2 students for the second role play.

B. *Role Play:* The students selected will enact the following scenarios:

– A group of students are walking to the bus stop. On their way they see a bag lying on the ground with something sticking out of it. One of the students stops to see what it is and believes it to be a handgun. The students discuss what to do with the gun. One of the students in the group uses the skill components to bring a safe conclusion to this scene.

– Two students are discussing the possibility of buying a gun because they think they need "protection." One of the boys knows where they can buy the gun, no questions asked. The two students role play the outcome using the skill components.

C. *Completion:* After each role play, the teacher will indicate if the role play was done correctly. If not, the teacher will ask the students to re-enact the role play with corrections. If the role play is done correctly, this activity is complete.

D. *Reinforcers:* The teacher will compliment and praise the students who participated in the role plays.

E. *Discussion:* The teacher will ask the students the following questions to start a discussion.

> ❱ **Why are so many people attracted to guns?**
>
> ❱ **What are the many reasons for people to think that they need a gun?**
>
> ❱ **Is there validity for these reasons?**

Students will explain how they can control their curiosity about guns and how to avoid being a victim of guns.

6. ***Practice:*** The teacher will distribute copies of the worksheet "Handguns" for students to complete in class and ask them to share their responses when they have completed the worksheet.

7. ***Independent Use:*** The teacher will hand out to students copies of the factsheet entitled "Children and Handguns" to share and discuss with their families and to learn what their families' feelings are on the topic. The teacher will ask students to write a few brief statements to describe the family reactions and also their own feelings, and bring these reports back to class in one week to share and discuss further as needed.

8. ***Continuation:*** The teacher will remind students of the power of guns and the serious consequences guns can cause when not handled properly and that even people who know how to handle guns can have accidents. He/she will emphasize that guns should be securely locked in a safe place, never looked upon as a toy, and never used to solve any type of problem situation.

Name _____   Date _____

HANDGUNS

Directions: Write a paragraph in response to each of the following items.

A. Give two reasons for the need to own a gun.

   1. _____

   _____

   _____

   _____

   2. _____

   _____

   _____

   _____

B. Contradict the reasoning above and make a valid argument against the need for owning a gun. Use the skill components. (The same argument might be valid for 1. and
2. If not, give two counter arguments.)

_____

_____

_____

_____

_____

_____

_____

_____

_____

_____

_____

_____

FACTS ABOUT . . .

Every day In America, 20 children ages 19 and under are killed in gun accidents, suicides and homicides. Many more are wounded.

(National Center for Health Statistics)

In 1989, 2,367 children and teenagers were murdered with guns, 1380 committed suicide with guns, and 567 died in unintentional shootings.

(National Center for Health Statistics)

Gunshot wounds to children 16 and under nearly doubled in major urban areas between 1987 and 1990.

(National Pediatric Trauma Registry)

In 1988, one out of six pediatricians nationwide treated a young gunshot victim.

(American Academy of Pediatrics)

Nearly half (48%) of all black teenage males who died in 1988 were killed with guns.

(National Center for Health Statistics)

One out of 25 high school students carried a gun in just one month in 1990.

(Center for Disease Control)

California schools reported a 200 percent increase in student gun confiscation between 1986 and 1990, and a 40 percent increase between 1988 and 1990. Florida reported a 61 percent increase in gun incidents in schools between 1986/87 and 1987/88, and that 86 percent of the weapons that were traced came from the students' homes.

(California Department of Education, Florida School Boards Association)

An estimated 1.2 million elementary-aged, latch-key children have access to guns in their homes.

(Center for Disease Control)

In 1990, gun accidents were the fifth-leading cause of accidental death for children ages 14 and under.

(National Safety Council)

An analysis of 266 accidental handgun shootings of children ages 16 and under revealed that 50 percent of the accidents occurred in the victims' homes, and 38 percent occurred in the homes of friends and relatives. The handguns used were most often (45%) found in bedrooms. Boys were predominately the victims (80%) and shooters (92%).

(Center to Prevent Handgun Violence)

Every six hours, a pre-teen or teenager commits suicide with a gun—nearly 1,400 in all in 1989. The suicide rate of adolescents quadrupled between 1950 and 1988, making suicide the third leading cause of adolescents' death. Guns are the leading method used by teenagers to commit suicide (60%).

(National Center for Health Statistics, Center for Disease Control)

Taken from the Center to Prevent Handgun Violence
1225 Eye Street. NW, Room 1150
Washington, DC 20005
(202) 289-7319